TWAYNE'S WORLD AUTHORS SERIES

A Survey of the World's Literature

Sylvia E. Bowman, Indiana University
GENERAL EDITOR

GREECE

Mary P. Gianos, Detroit Institute of Technology
EDITOR

Archilochos

(TWAS 59*)*

TWAYNE'S WORLD AUTHORS SERIES (TWAS)

The purpose of TWAS is to survey the major writers —novelists, dramatists, historians, poets, philosophers, and critics—of the nations of the world. Among the national literatures covered are those of Australia, Canada, China, Eastern Europe, France, Germany, Greece, India, Italy, Japan, Latin America, New Zealand, Poland, Russia, Scandinavia, Spain, and the African nations, as well as Hebrew, Yiddish, and Latin Classical literatures. This survey is complemented by Twayne's United States Authors Series and English Authors Series.

The intent of each volume in these series is to present a critical-analytical study of the works of the writer; to include biographical and historical material that may be necessary for understanding, appreciation, and critical appraisal of the writer; and to present all material in clear, concise English—but not to vitiate the scholarly content of the work by doing so.

Archilochos

By FREDERIC WILL

University of Iowa

Twayne Publishers, Inc.   ::   New York

*To the Parian butterflies
and the one among them
which is the soul of
Archilochos*

Preface

Archilochos appears to be our contemporary in many ways. Recent and fairly accurate translations of his work by Guy Davenport were reviewed favorably in *Poetry* magazine. In the preface to that translation, Mr. Hugh Kenner was able to say: "Mr. Davenport's Archilochos, cursing despite scholarship's rags, is a contemporary poet. . . . He has been made possible by our ability to engage the imagination with the pragmatic, by our renewed pleasure in the laconic and the expletive functions of language, and by our present willingness to assimilate these pleasures into our notion of Hellenism." Yet, when it comes to a scholarly book about the poet, it is not quite so easy to achieve this kind of presentation.

Archilochos did live a long time ago. Much of his work exists now only in cruelly mutilated fragments. What is worse, the pieces are bewilderingly hard to fit together. Different editors propound different theories of synthesis: from those of the French scholar Ferdinand Lasserre, who takes risks to bring together Archilochos' fragments, to those of Theodor Bergk (a remarkable philologist), who joined the fragments only on intuitive evidence. Deciding among such theories is no simple matter. Yet one's entire picture of Archilochos is likely to depend on the decision about proper arrangement of these fragments. Ancient identities are fragile.

Nor is this the only hindrance to a confident and reliable bringing-up-to-date of Archilochos' experience. We don't know what his poetry sounded like. We don't really know to what kind of background his lyric pieces were performed. We don't know how religious he was being when he made his various allusions to the cruelty of the world; they could have sprung from a god-filled or from a godless mind. We don't even know when he was being funny.

The work of the classical scholar, I take it, is to attempt to answer such questions, and to do so in the language, and to the ear, of his own time. I have tried to do just this—tried, I hope, as hard as Davenport did in his translations. But I have been rather uncomfortably aware all along of attempting to square that effort with an effort toward fidelity to the historical problems.

I have tried, first of all, to include only historical background which is strictly relevant to Archilochos' work; and even in doing that I have opened with a rather long caveat on the difficulty of arguing at all from life to works. I hope that my effort at using knowledge has not turned out to be inconclusive.

From Archilochos' work, second, I have rather carefully selected those fragments around which his inner history, or range of being, seemed to be expressing itself. (This collection coincided, on the whole, with the best-known poems.) That inner history I have taken existentially, or in terms of the different modes of expression in this poetry, rather than chronologically. For that reason I say here, "inner" history.

Like Davenport, I have decided to make my own translations of the poems and fragments I use. In this way I have at least been able to stress the points which I found most important in the Greek. (At the same time, we all know, missing the way the Greek reads.)

I have omitted a good many poems from consideration. The omission has not implied evaluation; I have not passed over poorer and kept better poems. In many cases evaluation would have been impossible; the fragmentary condition of the poetry prevents anything more than a neutral account. So I have chosen the poems as much on the grounds of *what* was said, as of *how* it was said. The purpose has been to give some unified sense of the character of Archilochos' extant poetic achievement; to stress, in the analysis of his presentations in language, relative degrees of sensuousness or intellectuality, and to suggest certain intermediate stages between those two extremes.

Finally, in the attempt at legitimate bringing-up-to-date, I have paid steady attention to the opinions and responses of others to Archilochos. This appeared the best method of showing the living energies of the poet. I hope not too much exception will be taken to my emphasis in the last chapter on the views of some twentieth-century German classicists. It would be a welcome marginal benefit, I think, if I helped in this book to make the works of some of these men better known in this country.

To points like the preceding a brief edifying conclusion, concerning classical scholarship, irresistibly attaches itself. It is no fresh conclusion, but it belongs here, and it belongs, I believe, to the spirit of this series.

The first age of philology is over. The possibility of a book like mine, admittedly, rests on the philological achievements of the last five centuries. To this point my bibliography is passing testimony. At that, it says little about the labor required to produce a text of Archilochos. That ground work has been the hardest—and most essential. More than the bibliography, I think, my last chapter salutes scholarship. Great German classicists of this century have broken new paths into the meaning of Archilochos and his age. They have spoken for spirit, but only after years of reading and analysis.

It can escape no one's attention that these active scholars are making a new demand on, and accepting a new demand from, Archilochos (and the Greek past generally). They are working out from learning and training, as will always be necessary in the study of the past, but they are working in terms of a fuller concern.

I say "in terms of "cautiously, because I do not mean to imply that they are working toward some edifying discovery through Archilochos. Rather they seem to me to be deepening their awarenesses as they study Archilochos and his age. I take this distinction to be rather decisive, and to deserve elaboration.

The notion of classical scholarship as inductive—or what the logic textbooks used to call inductive—established itself early in the game, already among the Alexandrian critics of Greek literature. In antiquity this kind of scholarship consisted, in fact, chiefly in the gathering of data, and was aimed generally toward putting together canonical texts. From 1500 through 1900 this activity was revived by professional students of classical antiquity, and on the whole—a wide generalization, but borne out by a look through Sandy's *History of Classical Scholarship*—carried out in the Alexandrian spirit. Bold new disciplines, like epigraphy, numismatics, indeed archaelogy, were established. Vast syntheses of facts were assembled, especially in the nineteenth century. But the spirit of mere fact collection continued to dominate, at least to dominate the professionals.

The year 1900 is no satisfactory date from which to mark a

change in this attitude. The nineteenth century had enjoyed too many men like Friedrich Creuzer, Erwin Rohde, and Fustel de Coulanges for us to write off its classicism as simply positivistic. In the same way, the period of work after 1900 has in many cases absorbed the barest inductive tradition of earlier scholarship, contenting itself with assemblage of data. Only this time, at this point, the inductive work has on the whole been more arid than before. The major soluble problems of ancient textual, historical, and archaeological data belonged to the past; there was little left to do except, like Browning's grammarian, "to settle hoti's business." Twentieth-century classical scholarship, especially in France, Great Britain, and America contented (and still contents) itself far too easily with the jejeune manipulation of details.

An idle half hour with the *Transactions of the American Philological Association* will convince doubters that in America this condition still prevails. Again, I ask the dubious to take on faith that continental philology, on the whole, is no more creative than is American. The large shift in philological engagement, which I discussed above, has of course been the exception, not the rule; everywhere, including Germany.

The breaking of the rule, I think, has been a natural enough product. Radical questions have been raised concerning the evolution within the development of classical scholarship, the purely inductive phase of which had used itself up, and concerning the greater engagement forced on scholarship of all kinds by a century in which the very existence of our culture, and the very possibility of scholarship about it, were threatened.

The noise of these double developments has not pierced all the ivory towers. Classicists build well. But it has been heard by a good number of concerned (and rightly self-interested) professionals, who, as I hope my last paragraphs hinted, have carried their inheritance forward with them. Among them, for several reasons, are many Germans; but Germany has had no exclusive rights in the matter. Jacqueline de Romilly, George Thomson, Norman O. Brown are among the numerous non-Germans, on both sides of the Atlantic, who have carried the burden.

The development of twentieth-century scholarship on Archilochos will have shown, in miniature, one line of this larger movement. The work of Bruno Snell, Werner Jaeger, Max Treu, and others has on this topic been philologically responsible. At the same time, however, it has been humanly deep and culturally creative. It is a proof, in miniature, both of the value of the previous philological achievement, and of the new values now incumbent on that achievement.

The usual array of obligations has gathered itself, and must here be pared almost to the usual bone. The German scholars, to whom I have just alluded and who will be discussed in the text, have given me new confidence in the importance of studying the lyric period of Greek culture; and to them, strangely enough, I feel almost my greatest debt. One of these scholars, Max Treu, has done me double service as a critic and as a translator of Archilochos. For some months I have had Treu's (now quite worn) edition within arm's reach.

Among other books, my critical bibliography will suggest where main debts lie. Geoffrey Hartman has, through the years of our rather peregrinating friendship, given me a number of ideas which have helped me in the use of scholarly books. And a few lovely days in 1962, spent with Kalliope Stavraki and the Staikos family on Paros, have helped me keep in mind that the work in my own book is about the real.

Betty, of course, really deserves the wreath.

FREDERIC WILL

Iowa City, Iowa

Contents

ARCHILOCHOS

by
FREDERIC WILL

Archilochos, the seventh century B.C. Greek lyric poet, is the oldest lyric voice preserved for us in the western tradition. He comes onto our literary horizon like a brilliant meteor of individuality after the impersonal world of the epic, which we had known from Homer and Hesiod. The present work opens by discussing the transition, in Greek culture, from "epic world" to "lyric world," a change which was broadly cultural, as well as verbal and stylistic. Then Archilochos' *distinctive* lyric individuality is introduced. Central chapters are devoted to the peculiar tension, in Archilochos' work, between sense-experience and semi-philosophical expression. The major fragments of the poet's work are thoroughly analyzed. The two concluding chapters assess Archilochos' influence and importance: first on the Greeks and Romans themselves; then on later scholarship. The Archilochos-theories of some twentieth-century German scholars are finally discussed; they are picked out for special attention, and for special admiration. These men are seen to have realized, in their discussions of Archilochos, the immense existential presence which that earliest poet still represents for any of us who read him wholeheartedly.

Chronology

CHAPTER 1

The Texts, the Man, the World

An inheritance of primitive, original power put him in a position to tear down the worn out ideologies of his tradition; and to open the way for a period of fresh and unencumbered naturalness. With barbaric roughness he completed the transition from the epic to the lyric age, and with Hellenic clarity he formulated this revolutionary break.

HERMANN FRÄNKEL, Dichtung und Philosophie

IN *The Birth of the Odyssey,* Jean Giono writes about a Casper Milquetoast turned hero. This mild man is returning home after ten years in the Trojan War. He is anxious for home, yet still close to the military experiences in which he has played a perceptive, retiring part. Tension between the extraordinary past and the normal future releases his one strong gift: narrative power.

Working his way across the Peloponnesos from east to west toward Ithaca, he spends his nights with shepherds. During the long after-dinner hours around the campfire, the wanderer relates stories about the war. He enchants and compels, building his own myth around him. He is central to that myth; he gives himself a mythical name, Odysseus, and tells how he devised, contrived, and slaughtered. His listeners become tired of hearing him.

At last he reaches Ithaca. His stories have grown topically around him. Rumors of his heroic return have preceded him from one sheep station to the next. Of this he is only partly aware; in his heart he is still a coward and, like every artist, will always remain one. But he has begun to sense his own power. He is confused; and as he approaches his house he becomes increasingly apprehensive. The apprehension of the suitors, who know he is coming, is even greater than his. Odysseus needs only to open the front door; the men run, terrified. The mild man has become a superman, the most potent creation of his own imagination.

I   *Relation of Life to Literature*

The relation between an author's life and his literary works is this complex. The work may reflect a highly distorted image of its maker. In recent decades we in America have been alerted to this kind of distortion. There have been frequent discussions of the "biographical fallacy," the naive assumption that the biography of an author provides a direct key to the meaning of his work. Older works of criticism, based on a reading of literature with that assumption, now seem completely inadequate to all except a few retrograde academics. So does the less familiar assumption that the individual creator directly reflects the spirit or public events of his historical moment. Only Marxists, and old fashioned ones at that, make this case. On all sides we find people hungering for texts and beginning again to value them for what they are.

Yet something unsettling reminds us that the work is still the man. Both terms of this equation are simply in process of redefinition. At certain moments of high criticism—Ernest Jones' study of Hamlet, Maud Bodkin's of poetic archetypes—it seemed that psychoanalysis could offer the fine concepts and vocabulary needed for a redefinition of one of the terms, man, and so for a fresh description of the relation between life and literary works. There is still some basis for this hope. But psychoanalytic criticism has never quite proved itself. It has remained abstract. Critics using psychoanalytic principles of criticism, as in the recently established journal, *Literature and Psychology,* discuss only general relations: man's struggle, say, to overcome the Oedipal situation as it appears both in him and in the literature he writes. However, what we need is a study of the relation of this particular psychic situation to this shaping in language; the relation and the differences between the way a psychic situation is worked through into *Oedipus Rex* and into Joyce's *Ulysses,* respectively. Language in literature is fused to a high stage of particularity. But psychoanalytic criticism, deriving from what aims to be essentially a "science," has been unable to stoop to the particular without losing its balance.

We are presently groping toward subtler, and more exact, statements of the relationships between author and text. (Sartre's biography of Baudelaire is a good example.) Recent psychoanalytic work is healthily dissatisfied with Freud's theory of art as wish fulfillment. The obliquity of the creative process is being freshly stated. We see that the author's psyche and social environment mark his work deeply: deeply, but indirectly, often perversely, like the mark of personality on a human being.

Little is known about the authors of ancient Greek literature. What is known is generally suspect since ancient biographical traditions were unreliable. When not suspect, as in many of the details known about Aeschylus, Aristotle, or Theocritus, these bits of evidence are so grossly external that they are useless for analysis of literature. It helps only very broadly to know that Aeschylus fought at Marathon, that Aristotle tutored Alexander, or that Theocritus passed some time in Alexandria. It is good to know when these men lived and what they did. But the more we learn about the obliqueness of the life-works relation, the more limited we find the ancient data, and the less appropriate they seem to be for any such analysis.

There is a hidden and double profit, for the classicist, in understanding this limitation of his materials. First, he is thrown back onto his texts. This necessity has usually meant, in the history of classical scholarship, that he is entirely reliant upon textual criticism or upon even more clearly ancillary studies—epigraphy, papyrology, archaeology in general. In other words, he has often let his limitation turn itself into pure limit, a pure disadvantage. But the classicist, more than other literary scholars, has had reason to feel guilty at such an evasion. This pretext for anxiety has been his first advantage. The second has been this: he has had none of the help provided—say to the scholar of Victorian literature—by detailed and pregnant biographical, or historical, information; *but, and as a result,* he has suffered few of the destructive temptations of rich biography and its many ways of making the scholar forget that the work matters more than the man. The classicist has ъeen forced at least to try using biographical data with finesse.

II *The Old Era*

What is known of the times and life of Archilochos is largely gross, in the above sense, and cannot by itself be expected to yield any profound understanding of his poems.[1] We must do our best, however, though dealing far more in data than in perceptions. A

kind of enrichment is possible by the simple contemplation of
these data. And at a more charismatic glance they may be seen for
what they are, apertures for classicists to see through.

No times are more appealingly (and appallingly) unclear than
those of Archilochos. He probably flourished in the mid-seventh
century B.C. and completed his life in the first two-thirds of that
century. Thus he lived at a time which textbooks, with approxi-
mate accuracy, call "transitional." One form of the old Greece was
giving way to the new. We must look at the old before we can see
the new.

Reliable estimates place Homer about a century before this
transition, toward 850 or 800 B.C., and at the end of the Mycenaean period. The Greece embodied in Homer's epics seems to be
a mixed conception inherited by him from several centuries of tale-
telling. Various strata of Mycenaean history are visible there. Yet
we sense that Homer is seeing evidence of vast development from
the rather massively feudal setting of the Mycenaean world. This
insight, we feel, is the force behind his greatness.[2]

The *Iliad* and *Odyssey* offer a picture of the social, economic,
and artistic conditions of life at a period of Greek culture some
centuries prior to Homer's time. Conditions are in many senses
feudal. The army before Troy and the society on Ithaca are
equally dominated by military landowners surrounded by their
retainers. There are few towns. Agriculture and fishing are the
main sources of wealth; but in this barter economy, wealth and
the accompanying power have gathered themselves in the pockets
of the kingly landowners.

Social relationships of that age are what we would expect. On
the vertical scale, men were separated by sharp class distinctions.
The lower class, constituted of men like Iris, the beggar on Ithaca,
or Thersites, the rabble-rouser at Troy, existed in a world different
from that of Hector or of Agamemnon. And "different" world
means "lower-class" world; a middle class did not exist. Men shar-
ing the highest level, however, were compelled by and did compel
a demanding code of behavior. There was heavy stress on honor
and a correspondingly inflated sense of pride. Rituals of greeting,
address, and thought development seem, even allowing for the
distortion of daily life in Homer's own ritual poetry, to have been
the governing tactics of daily behavior.[3]

The art of Homer's own time is likely already to have differed vastly from that of the various epochs whose experience is en-shrined in Homeric epics. We know that many of the artifacts of Troy, Mycenae, Argos, and other epic sites, important before the first millennium B.C., were elegant and precious. And we know that by Homer's own time, if 800 B.C. is a reliable date, a sterner visual art, geometric, was in charge, at least of ceramic tradition. Of Greek architectural or sculptural tradition during these periods, it is hard to speak. Only the smaller artifacts fit together intelligibly, if variously, to suggest the older world. The Mycenaean artifacts display a kind of unselfconscious sumptuousness reminiscent of the ancient Near East. The bare strictness of the "proto-geo-metric" work, the creations of eighth-century potters, call to mind a purely decorative, and highly ancient, Far Eastern or Persian work.

The world reflected or remembered in Homer's work, and al-most nowhere else, was in many ways ripe for change by the be-ginning of the eighth century; but I offer only the sketchiest per-spective onto that change: a few symptoms, no underlying causes.

Huge colonizing energy had settled Dorians in the Pelopon-nesos, and Dorians, Ionians, and Aeolians in Asia Minor around 1000 B.C. These were the great wanderings which directly fol-lowed the breakdown of Mycenaean culture, and which went into making temporarily more settled, and for the first time properly "Hellenic" civilization, as we know it from fifth-century Greece. Homer himself lived near the end of this period of cultural growth.

Though he writes of "events" long, perhaps four centuries, past, he finds in them thrusts and energies which were part of the new world opening at his time. The marine adventures of Odysseus and his company, and the quest for the spiritually new, with which both Achilles and Odysseus are preoccupied, make "real history" in the new colonizing movements of the eighth century and were to affect the Greek mind permanently.[4]

The aristocratic culture of post-Mycenaean Greece had already taken some steps toward what would later be called democracy. Early forms of the *polis,* the classical city-state, existed; society was no longer feudal in the Homeric sense. While there was still no middle class, there were possibilities—say of living from trade on land or sea—which promised looser, more money-centered so-cial arrangements. And even with that loosening there was serious discontent. Overpopulation on the mainland, reports of golden land overseas, and new senses of initiative drew forth a colonizing exodus from the Greek mainland, which began in the mid-eighth century. It was to create the idea of Magna Graecia—which filled Alexander's imagination—and to enlarge the Greek mind. It was also about to fill the Greek pocket and the Greek stomach. Settlements went out in all directions, carrying the hearthfires of mother *poleis* to the Black Sea, to southern Italy, and to Sicily. The Greek which is still heard in parts of Apulia was then heard all over the Mediterranean. Archilochos' life, we will see, was much affected by one of these movements.

A crucial discovery accompanied this enlargement of the Greek world after the discovery of money in the eighth century. Lydia, under King Gyges, was the first Greek state to coin money. (This is the Gyges of proverbial wealth, whom Archilochos mentions as a contemporary or near-contemporary.) The first coins were made of electron, gold mixed with silver. In rapid succession, many city-states established their own mints and adopted a silver standard. The older barter system, in which heads of cattle were norms of measurement, was gradually replaced, a replacement necessary in a culture relying increasingly on import and export, and in general on inter-*polis* communications. This large change was also much more than convenient. It fostered, and was fostered by, a new social mobility that not only broke the chains of the old feudalism but also those of the nascent *polis* system, which had at first been largely mainland Greek. Along with this mobility occurred, gradually but inevitably, a social leveling. Money eventually makes democracy possible; money can change hands, since it is acquired or lost, more easily than property and possessions; it can be manipulated by governments, even by governments of small city-states, for the common benefit (or harm).[5]

The mobilizing and releasing trends of social existence, which had set in vigorously by the eighth century, had impressive counterparts in thought. For us, Thales, Anaximander, and Anaximenes, all apparently born within the last twenty-five years of the seventh century, seem to spring from nothing. But they cannot have arisen so quickly. There have been theories about the Homeric, or more generally the epic, sources of Milesian natural philosophy, that philosophy for which air, fire, and water, respectively, were essential. The linking of Homer to that world view may be misleading and strained, for in many ways it ignores the spirit of poetry and of the way poetry contains concepts. But the audacious natural scientific metaphysic of the Milesians must somehow have been slowly prepared. Already, early in the seventh century, during the years of Archilochos' youth, this struggle of thought must have been under way. Though it seems to have confined itself to Asia Minor, it shows affinities to the larger movements of the post-Homeric Hellenic world. It is the most promising first harvest of that new world.[6]

III   *The New Era*

Changing social, economic, and intellectual traits marked the already developed form of this new world in which Archilochos was born. He is one of the first verbal sources of evidence from (and about) that world. Fortunately, for our understanding of this development, we have an important post-Homeric writer who prefaces much in Archilochos—Hesiod, who probably reached maturity around 700 B.C.

As a farmer who remained tucked in the shadow of Boeotian Askra, Hesiod removed himself from the broadly characteristic features of the new age, but in various ways he appropriated the new spirit of individualism which lies at the core of the post-epic, post-Mycenaean world-view. This new position Archilochos assumes more firmly, but with similar gesture, some two generations later.

Coming from Homer, the Homeric hymns, or from older Near Eastern literature like the Gilgamesh, we instantly see the new man both in the persona which Hesiod projects into his poetry and in what we take to be the Hesiod who made the poems.[7] In either case, the impression is of a crusty, Vermont farmer-theologian. Hesiod knows his limits and believes in limits. He knows what justice is and will fight for it. And he is full of wise sentences.

In delineating his own ideas and attitudes, Hesiod takes an unprecedented step into the light of world literary history. He uses the word "I," and he thereby gives us the sense that, for all his conservatism of thought and prosody, he is a revolutionary. Homer—according to Friedrich Schiller—was present in his creation in the way God is present in His: diaphanously, omnipresently, anonymously. Hesiod signs his name.

IV   *Archilochos as a Literary Man*

A couple of generations later—perhaps around the mid-seventh
century—Archilochos reached his own maturity as a writer. He
was to share the atmosphere of his world much more fully than
Hesiod and was to live with its movement. In broad terms, however, he resembled Hesiod in cutting himself off from much that
was anonymous and formal in the epic world.

Of facts about Archilochos we have some.[8] That he was Parian
has been confirmed and reconfirmed by archaeology, most recently by the discovery of a Parian dedicatory inscription which
speaks of a shrine and of a local cult of the poet. After his death,
he became an honored native son. His own, now fragmentary, text
tells us two fairly certain details of his early life: that he was a
bastard, and that he suffered a serious disappointment in love. His
legally binding engagement to a young Parian girl was probably
broken by her father (or by someone else). Then, as part of a
Parian colonization move, he appears to have gone to Thasos.
This detail we must take on faith, as far as I know. There is no
material evidence outside of Archilochos' texts. He may have gone
first to Siris in South Italy; he compares Thasos to it unfavorably.
As a young wanderer, he may have sampled Mediterranean ports
of call. What he did on Thasos or after it is all guesswork. Some of
his lines, and an ancient biographical tradition, indicate that he
died fighting against the Naxians, the perennial enemies of Paros,
a likely death for the man who put (or says he did) service to the
god of war on a par with service to the god of poetry.

This life unmistakably reflects, in certain ways, the world in
which it was taking place. Within the course of this life, a literary
persona, because surely in some sense also a real person, emerges
which is unquestionably part of the new world. That persona, Archilochos' personality in his poetry, is a literary personality which,
like Hesiod's, serves at least as its author's personal representative
and as the bearer of private, distinctive, even idiosyncratic attitudes. The Archilochos who finds his way into the poetry is in
many ways a reflection of the world in which that poetry was
written. The embodied personality shares much of the kinesis,
vigor, irreverence, quest, violence, and longing of what we take to
have been the epoch.

Question begging should be avoided, however, after the opening good intentions of this chapter. The relation to Archilochos' poetry of his life and times, as I have sketched them, remains uncertain: each half of the equation is incomplete in such a way as not quite to mesh with the other. (Even the external conditions for critical judgment seem to be lacking.) Archilochos' poetry appears to reflect, no matter how indirectly, at least projections of energy which were central to his life. He creates for himself the image of a person totally open to experience; he is a soldier-poet, a wanderer. Yet he is alternately ironic, bitter, funny, passionate— all in appropriate meters. In very broad external terms we know that his life has been an ingredient in his poetry. But his poetic artifice puts us on our guard. It makes us face the classical critical question: precisely how is *this* art reflecting *this* life? I will come back to the substance of the problem later, when it seems more appropriate for discussion. It is a tiresome caveat, at this point, that Archilochos as a man translated into his poetry is not simply Archilochos the man. But in final assessment this caveat will seem to be an important piece of critical caution and will take us a step closer to understanding our critical limitations.

CHAPTER 2

A Man from the Senses Up

> World history pales in comparison to what occurs in
> his [Archilochos'] own immediate ambience.
>
> HERMANN FRÄNKEL, Dichtung und Philosophie

THE emergence of a whole personality from the impersonal
world of Greek epic is momentous. We will later be able to
discuss even the metaphysical implications of the change. History
at this point seems tempted to convert itself into something more
than history.[1]

Before launching into the change, however, it will be helpful to
survey the historical bonds which continue to attach Archilochos,
as writer, to his past. Tradition was strong in the Hellenic literary
world, as it was in most literary worlds which flourished without
writing, and thus depended heavily on oral tradition.[2] We begin
now to suspect, in fact, that the Greek tradition may in many
ways have continued Near Eastern—Babylonian, Assyrian, Egyptian—literary traditions. Linguistic discoveries at Pylos indicate a
close Greek-Minoan-Phoenician affiliation.[3] A close look at the
Gilgamesh epic suggests baffling parallels to the *Iliad*. (Some of
the best Egyptian literature—Dialogue of a Man with his Soul or
the Story of Sinuhe—foreshadows themes of tension, anxiety, and
suspense to which the Greek tradition may well be heir.) And it
would in fact be surprising if Archilochos were *not* walking in
fairly well-trodden literary footsteps.

I *Prosodic Precedents*

Metrically, there were precedents for one of Archilochos' seemingly most daring innovations: that of interspersing hexameter
lines with briefer trimeter lines. This had already been done—we
suppose by Homer—in the buffoonish satire, *Margites;* and on
some of the earliest tomb inscriptions, which occasionally show a
pentameter line squeezed in among the hexameters. It is also

likely that much of the work of Kallinos of Ephesos both preceded Archilochos' work and encouraged him by example to take interest in asynartic verse-possibilities; that is, in writing poems with lines of unequal length. The epic hexameter was by no means the only existing verse form. To judge from Archilochos' highly skilled handling of the form, he must have apprenticed his ear to many masters of it.

But it is not a question here only of metrical precedents. There has been a veil of authorial impersonality over much in the epic tradition. Homer, and Hesiod only slightly less, conceal themselves carefully behind their language. Hesiod, especially in the *Works and Days,* emerges to address, bluster, and harangue his brother Perses in a way that anticipates Archilochos' assault on Lykambes, or more generally his addresses to "fellow-citizens" or friends. So this kind of poetic emergence, in Archilochos, is not unprecedented. Nor is the more broadly iambic mood, that quickness to assault, for which antiquity later knew and oddly dreaded him. The *Margites,* and various pre-Archilochean lampoon poems—like those attributed to Cercops—were apparently "iambic" in this way, full of harsh wit and obscenity. So also were those various poems, written at the time of Homer but remaining now only in ruined fragments, which a German scholar has termed *"eine reiche Fabel und Schwankpoesie . . .* ("a poetry rich in tales and jests").[4]

Iambic mood was in Archilochos, as in those who preceded him, close to the religious. In Homer's "Hymn to Demeter" (202 ff.), the cult of the goddess seems intimately related to the origin of the iambic verse form. There may have been some prosodic influence on Archilochos precisely through this cult. We know that the island of Paros followed an old Demeter-cult, and we suspect that Archilochos' family may have been occupied in the priestly service of that goddess. It is of parallel interest, though hard to interpret, that Archilochos refers to himself in one of his fragments as having led forth the "meters" or "dances" of Dionysus. All these religious embeddings of his verse confirm our sense that he was working in traditional channels.

II *Archilochos as a Modern Poet*

What strikes us more than any of this, however—and particularly in light of these traditional relationships—is his newness. In the perspective of world literature it is the differences of Archilochos from the earlier world, and especially from Hesiod and Homer, that interest us. As earlier hinted, this is most striking in the case of Hesiod. He employs the first person singular pronoun occasionally and constructs his work around a coherent personal philosophical attitude. He goes far beyond Homer in intimacy of mode. Yet at heart he is almost autochthonously old. When he writes of the ancient struggles of pre-Olympian theology or of the wisdoms of the mariner, he puts us in touch with the world of ancient Mediterranean experience. In terms of attitude, Homer is far more modern than Hesiod. (More modern, possibly, than anyone who has ever written.)

Archilochos is in every sense more modern than Hesiod. Not only does he project a more clearly and broadly delineated human figure into his poetry, but he views his world from an infinitely wider aperture. He is existentially open to that world from the senses up, while Hesiod meets his world in a predefined manner with his own dark, ancient, precautionary consciousness. In fact, he hardly meets the world—what we might like to call the real world—at all.

Sound tells part of the story of these differences. It is important that Homer and Hesiod, as well as Lucretius and Vergil, lived in the world of the dactylic hexameter. We are far from the sound world of epic experience; for that matter, we are far from the sounds of poetry at all. We have difficulty surmising how Milton sounded and are easily put off by him, led lightly to accuse him of being too sonorously and hypnotically musical. What, then, should we think about the music of an epic like the early Greek, which was accompanied by the music of the lyre and distributed into long, endlessly self-resounding, formulaic lines? The music of an epic might sound to us more like song than poetry. We would certainly find that the neutral contours of the poetry did all they could to hide the specific shape of the creator behind them.

Archilochos translates himself much more directly into his prosody. His poetry, too, was performed to the lyre and had its origins, evidently, in ancient traditions of sound organization. Just what these were, in his case, I have indicated as specifically as I could. Lyric poetry emerges after the epic tradition is spent, and yet hardly seems to derive prosodically from the epic. The asynartic alternation of longer with shorter lines in the various forms of

Archilochean lyric shows little relation to the relentless expanse of dactylic or epitaph literature. In the hands of an Archilochos asynartic verse was able to yield, almost as sound, what seems to be the sinew and texture of the poet's hearing and of the sounds in his own inner ear. Naturally, we feel more at home here.

III   *Sound in Archilochos' Poetry*

To explain the relation of Archilochos' sound to Archilochos as a man would exceed the powers of language to describe literature, even if we knew more about Archilochos the man. Such relationships can at best only be felt, even when an author's identity is well understood. In the present case, we must touch with lightest fingers. The predominant units of sound in Archilochos' projection are iambs and trochees. Reading for sound alone, we feel them more diaphanous revelations of their maker than are dactyls. I transliterate, for iambs:

> Psychás echóntes kýmatón en ángkaláis[5]   (Fr. 23)
> (They held their souls in ocean's arms)

> Anáx Apóllon, kaí su toús men aítioús
> semaíne kaí spheás / ollý' hósper óllyeís.   (Fr. 27)
> (My lord Apollo, point the guilty out
> and ruin them as you ruin.)

For trochees:

> Hós Panéllenón oídzus és Thasón synédramén.   (Fr. 52)
> (So the wretchedness of all the Greeks
> had come to Thasos)

> Ó lipérnetés polítai, táma dé xuníeté
> rhémat.   (Fr. 50)
> (Homeless fellow citizens, now grasp my words. . . .)

And, as a suggestion of the dactylic strategy:

> Ménin aeíde theá, Peleíadéo Achiléos
> oúlomenén, he mýri' Achaíois álgea ethéke,
> póllas d'íphthimoús psychás Aidí proiápsen

héroón, autoús de helória teúche kynéssin
oíonoísi te pási, Diós d'eteleíeto, boúle,
éx hou dé ta próta diástetén erisánte,
Átreidés te anáx andrón kai díos Achílleus.[6]

(Sing, goddess, the anger of Peleus' son Achilleus
and its devastation, which put pains thousandfold
     upon the Achaians,
hurled in their multitudes to the house of Hades
     strong souls
of heroes, but gave their bodies to be the delicate
     feasting
of dogs, of all birds, and the will of Zeus was
     accomplished
since that time when first there stood in division
     of conflict
Atreus' son the lord of men and brilliant Achilleus.)
          (Translation by Richmond Lattimore)

The emphatic energy, the nervousness of the shorter units in Archilochos, suggest the aural-sensuous makeup of a living man behind them, though in isolation from their meaning these sound units take on no specific identity. The suggestion of makeup is probably given by the relatively conversational tone of these iambs and trochees. They sound as though they might have been spoken.

It is certainly of some importance, as well, that the lines are few. Archilochos' work is badly mutilated, but it seems clear from what we possess, from the available statements and commenced parabolae of meaning, that he wrote nothing long. So there is, quite crudely, no chance for his iambs and trochees to repeat themselves like incantations. Everything here that might resemble ritual sound, totally patterned and alien to speech, is absorbed into the immediate flow of the argument. The sound of the beginning of the *Iliad* seems to say: I flow like Nature which will never stop and never change, despite the endless variety of the events it includes; I am, above all, not nervous. I have time! (How much work must go into changing man-as-man before sound, with such implications, can come from him!)

The living quality of Archilochos' language is made more obvious in his epodes, the ancient word for those asynartic poems in which he combines lines based on differing sound-units. Usually, as in the form perhaps established by him and later called elegiac, he combines a dactylic hexameter line with a second line composed of two two-and-a-half dactyl units:

> Eími d'egó therapón men Enýaloío anáktos,
> kaí Mouseón eratón / dóron epístamenós.   (Fr. 1)
>
> (Servant I am of the god of fighting
> and know the glycerine gift,
> gift of the Queens of all song)

The asymmetrical couplet has the energy of closed language, but it runs none of the dangers of Pope's slickness. This Greek remains close to the sound of life as it has been experienced.

What about these sound units considered as sounds bearing a meaning? (My analysis at this point still remains short of the question of meaning.) Iambs, as the ancient tradition believed— pointing to the verb *iambo,* to assail—can carry an invective weight, and in Archilochos they often do. Fate seems to have deprived us of many of those angry poems which in antiquity were considered the trademark of Archilochos. But we still have:

> Ouk án myroísi graús eoús' eleíphetó.   (Fr. 31)
> (Though she was old she didn't bathe.)
>
> Kat' oíkon éstropháto dýsmenés babáx   (Fr. 33)
> (Throughout the house a wretched babbling coursed)

and a few others similar to these, in which the oral movement of the iamb outfolds naturally into the intended attack. It is no vague impressionism, I think, to insist that the iamb in Archilochos is peculiarly suited for conveying such feelings.

This does not mean, certainly, that the trochee would not serve as well. But brevity of unit is what counts. Anger, often even sarcasm, comes in short breaths. Trochees do similar work in the lines quoted above: "Hos Panellenon oidzus es Thason synedramen," and "O lipernetes politai, tama de xuniete." In

Eí gar hós emoí genoíto cheíra Neóboulés thigeín   (Fr. 71)
(How I wish I could touch Neoboule's hand)

they fit themselves into gentle passion; while in

Kaí peseín drestén ep áskon kápi gástri gásterá
prósbaleín meroús te mérois   (Fr. 72)

(And to fall upon her, belly on belly
Meeting her thigh to thigh)

they carry their share—almost outworking the meaning—in conveying the angry thrust of passion.

This by no means intends to say that Archilochos confined himself to expressions of strong feeling. Where he does, his meters
work for him, translating intense, human energies. Where he phi-
losophizes, or suggests, his prosody holds to the contour of his
feeling, but in a way which is less easy to analyze and describe.
That metrical point will be made clear in the course of the following analysis of the fragments.

IV   *Content as Themes of Feeling*

Separations of form from content are evil, but they sneak
behind the scenes of even the best patrolled discussion of prosody.
By exposing trochees, iambs, and dactyls to purely aural attention
I meant only to ask for a temporary suspension of knowledge, the
knowledge that poetry is never sound alone. So I asked permission
to do what discussion of poetry must often do. Later, I will close
the artificial wound in the body of poetry. At the moment, however, I must inflict another wound, or rather keep the first one
open. I must talk about content.

It can be said at once, to mitigate the crudity of this program,
that with Archilochos, content, in the sense of subject matter, is
almost nonexistent. There are themes of feeling—of military
vigor, erotic passion, and bitterness at the cruelties of nature—but
he is not writing about anything specific. In this, he resembles
most of the Greek lyric poets.

Mainly for this reason I make no effort to discuss the matter of
his poetry in chronological order, in line, that is, with the temporal sequence of his life. Negotiation with the outer world is of

concern in this poetry, and Archilochos does not write about himself. But such negotiation is existential, not narrative, not an account. What seem to be significant in Archilochos are certain kinds of awareness which repeat and reinforce one another. If we had a full record of his writings, we might discern the development within kinds of awareness. As it is, we are safer, and truer to what appears to be the vision of Archilochos, if we study his clusters of awareness.

V   *A Poet of the Senses*

"A man from the senses up," I have called Archilochos, considering not only the prominence of aural energies which rise from bodily excitement and speak to the body of the hearer or reader, but also the sensuous as a realm of concern. What about "things" in his poetry?[7]

His finest picture is this:

> She held a branch of myrtle and
> Flowering rose and down her back
> And shoulders flowed shadowing hair.   (Fr. 29)[8]

This qualifies him as one of that small company of poets for whom Théophile Gautier said, "le monde extérieur existe," ("the exterior world exists").

The operative faculty here is sight, the most intellectual of the senses. The notions of seeing and thinking were closely related in the Greek experience. Homer had many words for different kinds of seeing: out of the corner of the eye, glaring, staring, and a number unnamed by us. There was an indication, already at that time, of the Hellenic responsiveness to the sensitivities of the eye. The words for idea, in Greek, reflect the act of seeing. *Eidos,* Plato's word for "Form," as in the *Theory of Forms,* is directly related to the verb *eido,* "I see."

Similar association is familiar to the western-language world, for which vision and insight are often the highest forms of perception, and for which no more natural language could be found to describe a Savior than "The Light That Came into the World." But the Greek association is even more intimate. Greek architecture (the Parthenon, Bassae, the Aphaia Temple at Aegina) and Greek sculpture (Attic korai, Kerameikos reliefs) prove this. In them, no matter is left to be mutely fondled by sight; each inch of stone opens out, draws in the eye, volatilizes into spirit. The first western mystics were literally "men seeing with their eyes shut," which is the meaning of the Greek word *mystai*. Such men had already made their appearance in the rituals and cults of Dionysus and Demeter.[9]

This may help to establish a way of understanding that Archilochos, a Greek for whom the exterior world existed, even in those poems where sense was operating most untroubledly, coerced that external world to a rare, aerial perspicuousness. There is in Archilochos none of that poetry of the tangibility of things which we find in various guises in modern poetry, as, for instance, in Wallace Stevens'

> Complacencies of the peignoir, and late
> Coffee and oranges in a sunny chair,
> And the green freedom of a cockatoo
> Upon a rug mingle . . .

or in Marianne Moore's

> trumpet-vine
> fox-glove, giant snap-dragon, a salpiglossis that has
> spots and stripes; morning-glories, gourds,
> or moon-vines trained on fishing-twine
> at the back
> door.

Even in these passages language becomes, through the strange density imposed on it, part of the visual experience which it evokes. (What is seen through words is always a function of syntax.) Yet there is in the Archilochos passage something characteristically aerial. The syntax seems to desensualize that which is seen.

Prosody has been partly responsible for the desensualization. In the pieces from Stevens and Marianne Moore the organization is fairly free, though ultimately mastered in a less formal sense. Like much of the best twentieth-century verse in English, this language is simply disciplined and pregnant conversation. Archilochos, as all the finest classical lyricists, writes a relatively regular, though infinitely nuanced, prosody. The disciplined regularity fights any unresolved sense-residues in the language. It can transmit limpidity, and even a Japanese haiku-like quality of verbal perception; but it can be only limitedly gritty, dense, or detailed.

It is worth making this general point in a day when few people enjoy contact with Greek or Latin texts, and when rampant, anomic poetic language is common in all but the most experienced poets. It is also the time to mention two details of early Greek prosody which reinforce understanding of the way in which Archilochos, in a passage such as

> She held a branch of myrtle and
> Flowering rose and down her back
> And shoulders flowed shadowing hair

removes the tangibility from the thing.

We are fairly ignorant of even the sounds of his language. What academic theory we have received, we owe to the highly inferential speculations of Erasmus. And at that, the Germans, English, French, and Americans all pronounce ancient Greek differently; not to mention the Greeks, who insist—and rightly at a few points —that their pronunciation preserves the ancient. Equally important, and relevant to my argument, is our alienation from the character of ancient emphasis. This alienation is vast. As any Anglo-Saxon traveler sees, the Mediterranean world is a gesture world. People talk with their hands. Even when they are talking to each other over the telephone, they gesture. The language used runs a dizzying gamut of pitch-points; it is indented by heavy stresses here and springs answeringly back there. The careful mastery of both pitch and stress provides a large field of esthetic operation for the skilled speaker of Greek.

Archilochos' concern with sense, in the myrtle-branch passage above, was the concern of a man living in an earlier, but in a presumably comparable stage of such a gesture culture. With his inner voice he nuanced. What we almost inevitably sound as stress in his words—as greater intensity of sound—he experienced only as length. The long syllables—the *chou* in e*chou*sa, the *tha* in *tha*llon, the *ter* in e*ter*peto—took a relatively long time to pronounce and were not necessarily pronounced more loudly or more intensely. The short syllables took less time to pronounce.

It can be seen that we have translated these terms from the time realm to the stress realm. We are thus unable to understand ancient pitch, which was the nearest ancient approximation to stress. It seems probable that in Homer the accent marks (acute, grave, circumflex) designated rising, falling, and rising-falling pitches of the reading voice. This is a likely theory, which would fit with the importance of instrumental music as background to the epic performance. And if it fits both Homer and Archilochos, it suggests a complicated set of tensions in the poetry of these men. Both pitch and length differentiations would be at work among sounds. Many syllables would be undergoing both pressures simultaneously. The *ter* syllable in the last word of Fragment 72's first line, *gastéra,* would endure both lengthening and pitch. It defies us to try to pronounce lines this way. Recorded attempts, as W.H.D. Rouse's reading of Homer, sound more like operatic recitative than they do like poetry. The subtlest case would occur in a rising-pitched, short syllable, like the *e* at the beginning of Archilochos' first line in the Neoboule poem: "Ei gar hos emoi genoito cheira Neoboules thigein" (see p. 32). Simply trying to voice the *e* while imagining a musical background helps to teach us how stylized this language was. And how far any perceived scene, transmitted in this language, would be from ocular density.

VI   *A Poet of Attitude*

The Neoboule poem of Archilochos is a highly refined sense presentation. A glance at some parallels may clarify the point.

Among the remains we will find few examples of even this degree of sensuous presentation. We begin to suspect that Archilochos is, above all, a poet of attitude, and only slightly less so of idea.

He has left:

Hýpseloús Megatímon Arístophoónta te Náxou
kíonas, ó megalé gái', hypenérthen echeís   (Fr. 17)

(Mighty those columns, Aristophoon, Megatimon:
Columns, my great mother earth, held in your
bosom today)

This appears to be a complete epigram, and so is reasonably to be considered a poem. It is sensuous by exclusion, to the degree that it fights off what seems an implication to express attitude. Wit, the pun on *kionas* (columns), is the point at which the sensuous and the intelligible meet and show the dividing line between them. On the sensuous side of the wit lies a half-felt immensity; on the intelligible side a kind of game and agility underlined by the poem's own aural lightness. That lightness is here dressed in elegiac weeds.

This kind of sensuousness, still short of attitude, appears in several places. In

> Álkibié plokamón hierén anethéke kalúptren
> Hére, koúridión eút' ekurése gamón (Fr. 18)
>
> (Alcibie who has offered the holy veil of her tresses,
> Hera receiving it now: maiden converted to bride)

we have perhaps the earliest example of what would later be the standard Hellenic dedicatory epigram. It is full of the genre's non-committal pregnance: in one sense, statement alone; in another, looked at differently, a strong implication that perhaps, "it was high time for the girl to marry," or that Hera, emphasized in the Greek by the run-on lines, is an extraordinary recipient of the gift. Other variations of emphasis, and according innuendo, are possible. The more we learn about an ancient poet's word-weightings, as in the use of Hera in these lines, the more subtle and elusive his language world appears. Perhaps the inner values shifted with the author's understanding and recitation, much as values shift in a modern lyric. In that case, the delicate interrelation of weights among the elements of an ancient elegy are the finest sense-carriers in the poem.

In Archilochos sensuous lucidity sometimes rests in a single detached line—a line once part of a whole, perhaps even of a philosophizing whole—which is now mere and poignant representation:

> Pros toíchon éklinthésan én palínskió (Fr. 34)
> (Against the wall they leaned in shadow)

The line is a poem in itself, in the way the best haiku or Tang Dynasty Chinese poems can be. (Though it was certainly not intended by Archilochos to stand alone, or to be looked at alone.) In sound and vocabulary the line testifies to acceptance of the world as it is. The simple mystery of this effect is inexhaustible. But the pathos and quality of human life, as far as they can be captured by organization of sense-awareness, are captured here.

CHAPTER 3

From Sense to Attitude

> *Thus we believe that a certain intelligibility mixed with a certain obscurity exists in every true work of poetry.*
>
> JACQUES and RAÏSSA MARITAIN,
> Situation de la Póesie

SENSE-experience as an ingredient in Archilochos' poetry makes a subtle topic. There are some preserved instances of limpid sense-experience in which the sensuous flavor of meter speaks into the texture of an expressed world, the world of the girl with the myrtle, of the columnar young men, and of the dedicatory Alcibie. But even in those cases meter works against sensuous density, toward the more refined sensuousness of *récitatif*, where the world of things has been carried far toward pure poetry. The subjects themselves have been lightened, turned toward play by wit—as in the column epigram: "Mighty those columns, Aristophoon, Megatimon: / Columns, my great mother earth, held in your bosom today"—or by innuendo. (It is at least possibly implied that the girl who "held a branch of myrtle" is a whore.)

I pushed the initial point, that of Archilochos' kind of sensuousness, to suggest that as a man of the new post-epic world, he was literarily operative as a whole human being, more so than Hesiod or, in one sense, Homer. It is no contradiction of this point to say that Archilochos assumes his new position also on a more complex level. The thrust, at the center of his sensuousness, was toward alleviation. In a larger sense it was toward attitude. The distance from seeing to point-of-view is not great. What ultimately compels us in Homer is his lack of point-of-view, or his control over what Schiller might have called the "divine" point-of-view. In Archilochos, we admire the coming into being of the first recorded secular, individual, Hellenic point-of-view.

Operations of sight are the point in Archilochos where we can best notice his seeing turning into, fusing with, or earning, his point-of-view. We begin, though, with a pair of more elementary examples, in which dark, half-tactile experience interweaves with attitude. (Attitude is essentially self-reflexive, thus the poems, in a way, are onanistic; they turn in on themselves.)

The first poem is:

> Wretchedly I lie desiring,
> Soulless, with an anguish from the gods
> Transfixed, clear through the bones.   (Fr. 84)

This is sensuousness without things. Even bones are dissolved into incarnate feelings. On the other hand, feelings are sensuous and sensible. Longing has become a sickness which infects bones, and which lays all flat and lifeless about it. This is a perfect dramatization of the physical-unphysical hypnosis of the lover who can't find his way out of love into action. The second poem is comparable:

> Such is the passion for love that has twisted its
>   way beneath my heartstrings
> and closed deep mist across my eyes
> stealing the soft heart from inside my body . . . (Fr. 103)
>   (Translation by Richmond Lattimore)

Like the first poem, this one may perhaps not be incomplete. (It is a characteristic of the early Greek lyric—alive wherever you touch it—that even its fragments seem entire). Like the first poem, this also preserves a sensuous-spiritual balance, even fusion, which is rare. We are used to poems about longing, the things longed for, and the feelings in the one who is longing; but we are unused to locating the feelings among the organs of the body. The heart is present as an organ, not as the metaphoric rhetoric-organ of which later languages, even later Greek, speak: as in our "take my heart," or "I give you my heart." [1] The mist poured over the eyes of the one who longs seems to bring its physical reality into the body of the poem.

When the breast is opened up, for the wits to be snatched from it, we suffer softly. There is no effect closer to this than that of

Sappho's famous poem, imitated by Catullus and read by experienced lovers ever since: the poem on her jealousy at another person's calmness in enduring the presence of her (Sappho's) lover. That person, who can endure such proximity, seems to her like a god: it would drive the poet's heart into her breast, strangle her voice. Her tongue would freeze, a light fire would run just under the surface of her skin, her eyes and ears would stop functioning, sweat (*idros,* a sweaty word) would run down her body; trembling would seize all of her, as she grows paler than sedge-grass. The effects described compel the reader to a physical projection which is rare in great poetry; and the more surprising in this, because the language is so highly formed. Being pre-Christian and unashamedly pagan, Archilochos and Sappho were somehow able to project physical awareness into language without softening the awareness into sentiment or straining it into prurience. Here we think of the undiscussable, self-adequate, self-equal presence of the human body in fifth-century Greek sculpture.[2]

I *Shift to Attitude*

In the two poems discussed above, sense-awareness and spiritual state were fused. In poems of scene, where the eye translates the I, Archilochos can be watched passing from sense-perception to attitude. We begin with a simple, fragmentary example:

> Ptossoúsan hóste pérdiká   (Fr. 106)
> (And crouching like a partridge there)

and then ask, for a second of academic privilege, to have the three words considered in themselves, as if they were a whole. They translate not only a position of the body, but a mood. The body is half-seen, half-felt where it is, through these words. Their vowelly sibilance holds, inexplicably, the secret of small, crouching animals; they are lonely but ready to skitter. The sensuously neutral is restless for a meaning which was no doubt directly at hand in the original whole.

In the following poem, statement mates syntactically with described sense:

> With incensed tresses and a breast
> that even an old man would have loved.[3]   (Fr. 30)

Again the activated sense is only partially sight. We see, smell, and feel the being, whereas earlier we only saw the girl with the myrtle. Next, "that" operates, quietly and grammatically proper, as both relative pronoun and introduction to a result clause, to show us one of the consequences possible to that sense-feast. The elected consequence is an expression of a minimal attitude toward the sexiness.

In the following poem, the same simple but poetically important progress is found in a different form:

> Like the spine of an ass this island
> Stands, with timber for a crown.
> Not a lovely or a wanted place,
> Or charmed, as one upon the banks of Siris.   (Fr. 21)

First we see, and that as clearly as possible. Again we notice how convincingly the external world existed for Archilochos. Many memories of harsh Greek spine-hills have been in the recipe for this language. It is impelled, prosodically, by a highly orchestrated gravity. (In Archilochos iambs do much besides assailing.) Then the poem, like a syllogism with middle term suppressed, moves to its conclusion. The logic of feelings takes on the guise of necessary logic. The guise is more illusory than in the preceding poem, because the "not," *ou gar*, in the island poem alone, does not introduce a consequence, but a state which is concomitant and reinforces that announced in the first two lines. It does not follow, from the look of mule-spined Thasos, that it is uncharming, that it is unlike the Siris river in Southern Italy. It is simply a fact, made sensuous and felt in the first two lines, and explicit in the last two. Attitude is implicit in the whole piece, but it is made more explicit by the last part.

In this light two more poems should be discussed, chosen because they present a different technique of organizing visual material for attitude. There is no longer the poetic syllogism of the "so that" kind; hardly even of the second, concomitance-stating kind. The first example:

> Glaukos behold, the heavy sea is shaken
> by waves and a vertical cloud stands
> straight at the summit of Gyrae;

a signal of winter; dread from
the unexpected arrives.   (Fr. 54)

Greek fear of the storm and sea is known. This poem appears at first sight simply to arrange powerful observed symbols for that fear. Then, at the word "winter," it repeats itself in more pregnant (though more abstract) language. There is no syllogistic development as the poem passes from what is seen to an attitude toward what is seen. Nor is there the kind of syllogism by concomitance found at the end of the poem on Thasos where "the wretchedness of all the Greeks had come to Thasos." Here we have a repetition of the point of the first two and a half lines which puts that point in a different, possibly even self-transcending, way. It is a mysterious accounting for a meteorological situation. If there is logical progression in this poem, we might call it a liturgical logic.

The last sight for the moment is this:

> I don't like the towering captain with the spraddly
>   length of leg,
> one who swaggers in his lovelocks and cleanshaves
>   beneath the chin.
> Give me a man short and squarely set upon his legs,
>   a man
> full of heart, not to be shaken from the place he
>   plants his feet.   (Fr. 58)
>   (Translation by Richmond Lattimore)

For the first time in these examples, attitude and perception are almost totally interwoven. (The poem is, in this respect, one of a small class.) True, the "I don't like," and the "give me a man short . . ." in the third line, make the author's evaluation explicit. He parades his prejudice.

Suppose those two clarifying remarks were missing and replaced by descriptive introductions to lines one and three? The poem would be almost unchanged; much less significantly changed than the preceding sight-poems would be changed by removal of their explicitness. In each of those, the explicitness—"even an old man would have loved," "no beautiful place like those near Siris", "fear comes from the unknown"—adds a great deal: either by limiting the possibilities for conclusion through

expanding the reference of the poem's sensuous detail, or by
drawing an awful pregnancy out of that detail. In the present
poem, all point is carried by the sensuous detail. The adjectives
used to describe the two kinds of captain express, in their respec-
tive combinations, the characters of the two men, the author's attitude in each instance having been part of his way of seeing.

II *Narrative Poetry*

All of Archilochos' poetry draws attention to its sound, and
must have done so far more compellingly in the ancient sense-
context. Furthermore, as we have already seen, a number of his
poems use sense-material, things seen or felt, as their raw stuff.
Yet, by one strategy or another, these poems turn themselves into
expressions of attitude. It may be that Archilochos is not unusual,
but simply human, in this thrust to leaven the sense-weight of
language.[4] (What else, really, is the whole tendency toward idea
in individual human development?) What is of interest here is the
particular way in which Archilochos performs his trick.

We can follow his projection of attitude from a different mode
of poetry, from narrative or rhetorical pieces, with their bases only
loosely sunk into a sense-foundation. For the first, we choose a
tiny example:

> Seven men fallen dead, whom we hammered with feet,
> a thousand killers we.   (Fr. 59)

This is a piece of story which at first seems harmless. The trochaic
meter runs unselfconsciously, not winking. Only a second later, in
this fragment of the original whole, do we get the heavy irony.
The attitude is a bitter laugh.

A little tale is often Archilochos' way into attitude. Take this
example:

> No great number of arrows will fly or rapid
> slings, when Ares crashes his war
> on the plain; the muchgroaned labor of swords will
>   rage.
> Of such a war they are masters,
> The spearfamed lords of Euboea.   (Fr. 3)

The story, propelled by regular distichs, is foremost and easy. Perhaps it was weighted with some implication which could be known only in context of the missing parts of the poem. However, as it stands, it is not without implication, it is not merely an account. The second line carefully dresses the War God in his most ominous role. Then the language, in the third line, grows densely cruel: the labor of swords will be "muchgroaned" (*polystonos*). The adjective is rare in early Greek. (Though of course we inherit only a fragment of early Greek literature and, in any case, have no way to judge the character of the period's spoken language, against which supposed oddities of written language must be measured in order to determine the total effect of any word.)[5] A sinister pressure is given back by the *daimones,* translated here as "masters," of the fifth line: the lords of Euboea are uncannily knowing, even demons at this kind of fighting. The poem began as a flat indication of what kind of weapon would or would not be used in a certain battle, but the thrust was toward the sinister weapon actually to be used. And the conclusion, as we have it, brought us into the hearts of the ones who will use the weapon.

What I call the rhetorical-narrative manner in Archilochos rarely reaches us so free of explicit comment as in the last poem. This situation may be only the accident of preservation. To the end of the third line, the following poem resembles the preceding in offering weighted but uncommented narrative:

> Come on, on the seats of the rapid ship
> come on and draw from the giant vats
> drink scarlet wine from the bung; who's about
> to stay alert on guard this night?   (Fr. 4)

There is a sense pervading the first three lines that the occasion of wine drawing is soon to be explained; even a feeling that it may be a strange or powerful occasion. In this, the drinking and fighting poems are comparable; we see in each the development of tension. In the present poem, attitude is not quite what emerges. Explanation, though, adds a kind of abandon which reinforces the earlier exhortations and becomes almost a way of looking at them.

My last two examples in the category also tell brief stories, but this time more meaningfully autobiographical. In the first, attitude is near the surface at every point:

> By spear my kneaded bread, by spear my wine
> of Ismaros, I drink leaned on that spear.   (Fr. 2)

This is a dazzling self-revelation: no tone can be imagined more
conclusively announcing the end of the epic voice. It is rapid narrative, moving over three poses, each struck briefly, kaleidoscopi-
cally, and the maker himself swaggering. Attitude seems so much
part of the poem that it is hard to imagine separation between
sense-material and elaborated point of view. The world of syllogistic poetry is sharply excluded. Something new in Archilochos
replaces it: a relation of the poet as maker, outside the poem, to
the poem he has made.

There is an irony in the present distich. We are forced back to
the kind of awareness Jean Giono elaborated in *La Naissance de
L'Odyssée*. Poets are generally not soldiers of the soldierly sort,
even when they can fight. The poetic effort, to make self-sufficient
presented objects, is totally different from the out-turning, prac-
tical movement of the soldier into his world. This limitation to
poetic stance may not have existed in Archilochos. (I don't pro-
pose psychoanalysis here any more than in the first chapter.) But,
undoubtedly, Archilochos the poet was aware (and especially in
his poetry) of a tension between the poetic and military attitudes.
He has embodied this tangible sense of strain: the orderly tight-
ness of prosody tenses off against the poet's flip ascription to himself of the military way. This embodied sense of tension is Archilochos' attitude toward his poem. It is attitude only in a slightly
new sense.

I have been concerned with a kind of evolution of attitudes,
from the fairly flat poem, on Megatimon and Aristophoon, or on
Alcibie, through more implicatory poems, "Glaukos see . . . ," to
somewhat direct statements of attitude, within the poem, as in
"Like the spine of an ass . . ." In the present distich, which still
moves out from sense, there is attitude, even swaggering attitude,
in the language. But the author's self-consciousness is also present
as attitude and works as a hidden ingredient in the language.

Something similarly complex holds for the next piece, which has
suffered equally for its invitation that we should consider it only
as an extraordinary document in Greek cultural history:

> A certain Saian delights in my shield
> which I left in a bush, not caring.

> I'm still alive thank god; to hell
> with the shield; I'll find me a better one soon.   (Fr. 6)

We are so possessed by the fluency of the offhand language that a close look is difficult. We stop with the obvious and the important: Archilochos throws away the heroic code with his shield. Homer and Hesiod do not even write about such characters or character. Although Homer is never guilty of a stylized heroic attitude, and Hesiod is in many ways simply a prudent farmer, still neither epic maker could imagine a flip and mercenary attitude toward a situation drawn from the heroic context. To refuse the game, in Archilochos' suggested way, had been impossible (at least in epic literature).[6]

The poem that works this wonder is again narrative, and puts us once more in the realm of syllogistic attitude. The tale is told, as elsewhere in these two-distich pieces, by the first two and three-quarter lines. Then an attitude is adopted toward the tale. It continues the tale which had at least potentially implied such a conclusion. (Though the vagueness of that potency is one of the poem's charms, giving the decisiveness of *erreto,* "let it go to hell," great and added punch.)

Again in this poem, as in the last one, attitude seems to be shed from outside upon both the narrative and the attitude within the poem. The narrator comes closer to us at the end of the poem. He addresses an unspecified audience, the neutral but presumably sympathetic and even intimate audience generally posited by the lyric voice. Strictly speaking, this was also the audience in the beginning, in the first two lines. But if we read and reread these lines, we realize that Archilochos is speaking to himself, perhaps breathlessly, in a kind of private retrospection. However, at the end, he is facing his audience. Archilochos the maker is, of course, larger than both these personae, than both these guises of distinctive address toward the audience. By introducing a break in the direction and tenor of his two assumed personae, Archilochos openly manipulates the poem in which he is acting. This experienced manipulation is essentially an attitude of Archilochos toward the attitude which he expresses in his poem.

III   *Fusion of Sense and Attitude*

The question of attitude has been introduced as a line along
which to guide a systematic analysis of Archilochos' poems. I will
want, finally, to give some sense of the spectrum of his self-
expressions, of the wholeness of his language-self. In analyzing
Archilochos, the main job is getting off the ground; showing with
some finesse, if possible, just how he himself moved from the expression and experience of sense-realities to a view of those
realities; how, in other words, he leavened his poetry. This is no
analysis of temporal development, of the evolution, in time, of
Archilochos' control over language. As I have said, too little is
known of Archilochos for that kind of inquiry to be worthwhile.
My interest has been rather in the essential character of Archilochos' poetry, not in its history. I have aimed at the ontology or
original structure of the work.[7]

Visual (and other) descriptions, and narrative-rhetoric poems
have been the chief specimens in this chapter. In each of these
types I have shown the emergence of attitude which, in the last
two pieces considered, seemed an increasingly complex concept. I
want to close the chapter by considering a small category of sense-
poem.

I am thinking of a kind of optative poem in which a wish for
sense-pleasure is expressed, and which shows, in perfect fusion,
the meeting of sense and attitude.

> If only I could touch Neoboule's hand.   (Fr. 71)

The soft, sensuous finality of the prosody and vowel qualities carries the sadness of feeling. The feeling itself is erotic-romantic,
intense but sublimated, in a way unparalleled elsewhere in Archilochos. (It is closer, by far, to a frequent mood in Sappho.) The
sensuous, really the sensual, is here leavened not by attitude, and
certainly not by idea, but simply by longing. Archilochos is generally willing, as he says moralistically in a few of his idea-poems, to
restrict his hopes to reality. Such optative poetry as the present
line is therefore rare. When it occurs, it can evidently turn sense
into sense plus longing and create a romantic poem.

Such longing, in Archilochos, is not only rare, but it gives a
delicacy of aspiration, as distinct from one of prosody and crafts-

manship, which has led some classicists to substitute other imagi-
nable words for the *cheira* ("hand") in Archilochos' line. Such
scholars have fewer textual temptations with this second optative
poem:

> And to fall upon her, belly on belly
> Meeting her thigh to thigh.   (Fr. 72)[8]

It is possible that Neoboule, lost temporarily or permanently, was
also the object of this wish.

The sensuousness of portrayal is heavy and forceful (in the
Greek, almost brutal). The general prosodic point holds: that
these trochees, lengthened and emphasized at their outsets, force
and drive the language ahead. They control the reader. But in
addition there is an extraordinary adjustment of the sensuous in
words to its achieved reason, to its prose sense. I mean through
the immediate repetitions of "belly," though (in Greek) in different cases, and of "thighs," though (in Greek) in different cases.
The desired falling of belly on belly, and the desired heaving of
thigh on thigh, are dramatized by the immediate, slashing proximity of the words for those two parts of the body. The slashing
force is strengthened by the use of datives for the particular
"thigh" and "belly" moved against. (I may be relying too heavily
on the exciting strangeness of such an inflected language. Perhaps
dative usage here, grammatically controlled in the Greek by the
prefix of *prosbalein*, to "meet" or "cast upon," would have struck
the ancient Greek ear as only neutrally natural.) The dative seems
to function as receptacle; "motion toward" seeming, therefore, to
imply a further, more desired, motion continuous with it.

Whether or not this grammatical point holds, the little piece
returns us to a starting point. From here it is worth thinking back
to certain poems discussed earlier: again to those on Aristophoon
or Alcibie, which, on the whole, seemed placidly visual; or to
those in which Archilochos was, as I said, onanistically bent over
the moods of his own viscera; to those poems, in short, in which
Archilochos seemed least to adopt an attitude toward his poetic
stuff. The second of the two optative poems achieves just this kind
of neutrality, but in a different way. It expresses a wish so mutely
(and eloquently) physical, and through language so adequate,
that it leaves no interstices for attitude.

CHAPTER 4

Ideas

*Idea is the form of things recollected by the imagi-
nation. . . .*

ÉMILE BERNARD

THE status of ideas in poetry is hard to describe. We realize
that the discussion of poetry in terms of form and content is
dangerous, and that the discussion of content largely in terms of
ideas or of the poet's beliefs is even more dangerous; in fact, it
makes a joke of criticism. It leaves the always essential sensuous
substratum (and middle stratum) out of consideration. It turns
criticism into freshman philosophy.[1]

To this point consideration has been given to the character of
Archilochos' poetry from the ground up, from his most sensuous
awareness, and presentations, to those poems, the matter of this
chapter, in which he most nearly troubled himself about what we
might call ideas. A weakness in method has followed me all the
way. I considered prosody in the beginning chapter, and have
continued to wave my hat at the topic. But increasingly, and even
more in the present chapter, I talk about poems as though they
were not, in part, radically mere sound, or sense-material, and as
though they were not part of an immediate, or rational historical
context. I have tried thus far to avoid referring to ideas, but I
have slipped into much talk about content.

This unavoidable violence done by the language of criticism to
that of poetry can be mitigated by an effort to see what I called
the spectrum of a poet's expression, and how it ranges from the
most to the least sensuous aspects of that expression. Insisting on
the sensuous ground of the things said, in poetry, is at least a kind
of running atonement for ignoring the sounds in which the meaning is said.

I *Poetry of Idea*

I begin this chapter, atoningly, with poetry of idea which best recalls the closeness of all Archilochos' poetry to the life of the senses. The poem tells a story and draws a conclusion:

> Nothing impossible is such
> no thing miraculous, since father Zeus
> sent out of noon a night, and shut the light
> of the brilliant sun; a wretched fear came down on men.
> Since then all seems credible to men, and hopeable.
> None of you now be startled, watching
> when beasts change nature with dolphins
> and fall in love with echoing waves of the sea
> and mountains are the sweetest home for fish.   (Fr. 74)

Except for a strangely grave tone in the first three and a half lines, this poem starts off with a familiar promise: to move from the particular to the general, to argue, as we saw earlier in the following two poems:

> Glaukos behold, the heavy sea is shaken
> by waves and a vertical cloud stands
> straight at the summit of Gyrae;
> a signal of winter; dread from
> the unexpected arrives.

> A certain Saian delights in my shield
> which I left in a bush, not caring.
> I'm still alive thank god; to hell
> with the shield; I'll find me a better one soon.

Yet, a caveat has been entered at the beginning of the eclipse piece; the puzzling suggestion that anything now is possible; a suggestion which, at this point, looks like stage-setting, while, in fact, it proves to be a wedge of the surreality which conquers at the end. Not only is personal attitude not being anticipated, as it is in the other two poems, but a strange heightening of the narrative events is from the beginning acquired in the present poem. The heightening, perhaps slightly ironical but still high style, prepares us for the final talk of a topsy-turvy world.

The final vision of inverted natures may (or may not) be taken as a move into the precinct of ideas. At its simplest level it is a conceit; and I see no reason to deny early Greek lyric poets a sense of word play; we are usually too strict with them.[2] Play words, like the "echoing waves" or the "sweet" in the last line, bear out such an interpretation. I prefer a slightly heavier view; and for this reason consider this as a poem of ideas.

The Greek word *nomos,* at the end of line seven, "when beasts change nature with dolphins," is a clue. Broadly, that word means "law" or "principle of order." In application to a genus of beings it will mean something approaching *telos,* "end" or "final cause." This is apparently what it means here. We are to expect a universe in which the appointed natures of creatures may be changed, even traded off. Genera will overflow those boundaries in terms of which they have their meaning. Meaning itself will flow loosely and as uselessly as spilled water through the universe.

The other poems to which I attend in this chapter are more direct in presenting the ideas they treat; they lie farther from purely presentational language. I begin, for the sake of clarity only, with two one-line gnomic examples. The first:

All things labor achieves for man, labor and mortal study.
                                                                              (Fr. 15)

and the second:

All things luck and fate, O Perikles, present to man.   (Fr. 16)

These are perfect dactylic hexameters, each cast in a strangely Ur-epigrammatical form. I feel, here, the plausibility of a theory: that the lyric may originally and then later in the early Renaissance have grown from the epigram, or in close affiliation with it. Epigrams are all the same in felt-form. The stunning difference between these two pieces is made almost unnoticeable by their similar surface radiances.

Neither poem arrests itself for specific sense-detail or for elaboration; yet the thrusts are forceful and opposite. The first poem ascribes all good fortune to human effort; the second, to luck and fate. Considering the two lines, for the moment, as philosophy, not as philosophy in poetry: is there a possible reconciliation between the two lines?

Archilochos is a philosopher close to nature; close especially to the violence of one expression of external nature, the sea; and to one internal expression, passion and rage. As he works with these two forces he becomes, at least as a personage in his poetry, increasingly aware of the degrees and ways in which men are unable to control their own destinies. (We may assume that the rage at losing Neoboule gradually converted itself into resigned acceptance of the exigency in life.) Fate and luck will have deified themselves slowly through experience. There will remain, at the same time, a sense of the importance of human effort. Men close to the sea or to their passions are likely to feel this too with the growth of their experience; they will feel that they must do all in their power to anticipate and control nature. On the other side of that prudence lies fatalism. This may not be the philosophy of the schools, but it is often the philosophy of philosophers in poetry. (Poetry and labor come close together here.)

I have no desire to prove Archilochos a philosopher or to build unimagined bridges among his often widely separated thoughts. The lines quoted above have in any case an unrepresentative, tantalizing relation to one another. Between them, though, they do suggest a range of concerns which embrace most of the extant philosophical remnants of Archilochos: that suggestiveness is our chief profit from the two lines.

At their center lies a concern with what I loosely termed nature, meaning to stress a force which puts man in mind of his limitations and of certain necessary controls. Harsh outer nature usually means the sea. Archilochos was born on an island, lived on islands; as always in the Aegean, those islands were small, shaven, and forever opening up prospects of ocean. Ships were only fairly strong, storms were frequent, and the sea was often a killer. We have one brief testimony from Archilochos:

> Let's hide the unholy gifts of the lord
> Poseidon.   (Fr. 10)

The "gifts" are the drowned bodies.

II *A Bridge Between Physics and Metaphysics*

The theme of drowned bodies is picked up much more elaborately in the following:

> The funeral groans, Perikles, no one of the citizens,
> not one small city can know in rejoicing;
> such are the men whom the wave of the echoing
> ocean had buried, leaving us pressure of pain
> at our hearts; but the gods, my friend,
> have given us mighty endurance of pain,
> medicament; now one, now another is struck.
> We groan with the bloody wound today
> in turn to be others': instantly
> push your effeminate pain away, and endure.
>
> (Fr. 9)

At the center lies the sensed cruelty of the sea. As often, the sea itself is not described; as often, the natural world existed for the Greek poet—Sappho, Alcaeus, Solon, too—as a genesis of human feelings. Archilochos' voice is very differently related to the world from the voice he assumed in "She held a branch," or "Wretchedly I lie desiring. . . ." The luck of text preservation may partly account for this feeling. In the present poem much is preserved, and perhaps the entire poem.

The whole esthetic structure—prosody, imagery—appears and, as always, somewhat interposes itself between the things experienced and the person who experiences them. But there is an irony in the tone of narration which does much to put the narrator's person in the foreground, in the front of what he is talking about. In the second line the "know in rejoicing," the "pain at our hearts" (literally, at our "lungs"), the exquisite placing of the word (in Greek) for medicament: all these studied turnings not only bring the author's persona into firm relief, but they suggest bitterness toward the sea, which is of more poetic interest than the sea itself. It is no surprise to find that in what is the end, apparently, the poet pulls out a familiar Stoic slogan. Archilochos is playing the soldier in his best manner. A caesura intervenes artfully, and with careful distributive power, between "effeminate" and "pain" in the last line.

Stoicism is an attitude in the face of both external and internal nature. It is a universal refuge of the instinctively unphilosophical mind when it is driven by personal experience to adopt some attitude toward life which will absorb shock. Nature forces that solution on Archilochos.[3]

Holding out is the core of Archilochos' Stoicism: the principle is defended on simple grounds, that human affairs change, and that man, unhappy today, will be happy tomorrow. We saw this argument before, and find it more prominent here:

> Leave all things to the gods; for often from evil
> they raise up men laid flat on the cobalt land,
> and often they trip the steady and firm
> on their backs; when evils in number arrive
> a man is beside himself, in lack of life.   (Fr. 56)

The feeling of holding out is dwelt on, but simply.

I have discussed ways in which the sensuous texture and objects of Archilochos' poetry are refined toward the more abstract exigencies of pure poetry. A new kind of example presents itself in the preceding poem where Archilochos works through a central, and almost mathematically demanding, equation. Upright stance is equated to being in prosperity, and proneness is equated to being in adversity.[4] Such metaphors, drawn from the physical world, are poetic commonplaces; but the metaphor in this case is so boldly, even baldly, equivalencing (I think of the rapid bodily ups and downs of slap-stick comedians) that the role of the physical world in the construction of the metaphor is forgotten. The precariousness of human affairs is so sharply dramatized that a move into theology earns its place at the beginning of the poem. This is not the only scrap of explicit theology in Archilochos, as we shall soon see.[5]

First, however, another example of Stoicism based on sense of flux, on a sense which the philosophers of Asia Minor were to examine metaphysically no more than a century later. The next poem courageously, but in purely poetic terms, sketches plans for a bridge between ethics and metaphysics:

> My heart, my heart stirred up by blocking griefs
> rise up, and cast your chest to block them
> bravely, and near your foes be safe

and neither in victory boast out open
nor beaten fall in weeping at home:
take joy in joys, and give in not
too much to evils: knowing what rhythm holds all men.

                                        (Fr. 66)

The last line is justly famous and has deserved much of the
discussion dedicated to it. The chief question has been: what is
rhysmos, "rhythm"? The question is important because the idea of
flux in human affairs is generally important in Archilochos—as in
the poems discussed above. It is also important because in some
way Archilochos seems to be pioneering or attempting for the first
time in the West to abstract from a wide variety of daily experiences to a notion of the nature of things. "Rhythm" is surely *not*
only the ups and downs of human life, sadness followed by joy,
followed by sadness. It is partly that. But, as in the previous
poems, we feel that those ups and downs are caused by the interaction of the outer world with the subject. Archilochos, the persona of these poems, is no manic-depressive: he reacts to details of
the outer world, sometimes to the sea, sometimes to his passions,
sometimes to what he collectively calls, as in this poem, the
"blocking griefs," sufferings for which no strategy of solution
seems to be at hand. Rhythm is the way the world goes where
world is the intersection of man, as subject, with the objects outside him. Archilochos here achieves a philosophical statement,
backed by the described texture of his own experience, which
moves out from passion, but testifies to an untroubled belief in the
existence of the real world. The special success of formulation in
this poem conforms to its especially delicate perception of the ethical situation, which follows from living in a rhythmic world.
There is some of the earlier and easier response found in the previous poem: know that your estate will change. But there is a new
turn: one should not give in to excessive sorrow, or to good fortune: he should simply know that these conditions will *not* last.

A kind of equanimity is finally preached, in the impressive
words "neither in victory boast out open." An evenness of understanding and temper is needed in order to conform to the rhythm
of what-is. This is perhaps a strange argument. Certainly it looks
forward to the Stoics, properly so-called, to men like Zeno and
Chrysippos, who occupied a firm world view in terms of which to

iron out such wrinkles of paradox. Archilochos is simply translating his own experience. His bridge between ethics and metaphysics is thus all the more remarkable. He sees quite nakedly, and perhaps mainly through the thought-prompting stringencies of his own art, the way in which what a man *does* is related to the nature of the world in which a man *is*. It is the deepest achievement in Archilochos.

CHAPTER 5

A Gathering of Fragments

Much, not many.
Greek proverb

A PICTURE has emerged from the analysis of the poems in the last two chapters, which, though incomplete at many points, makes Archilochos appear more than usually versatile in lyric-poetic terms. What he is saying in prosodic language varies from the thickly (or rather violently) sensuous, through the subtly, often ironically attitudinal, toward the metaphysical, a highly refined and general perception, as in the last poem discussed, into the character of being. The range is wide, even rather balanced. But the balance can be deceptive in one particular way. The language which displays this wide range is itself highly sensuous and must have been far more sensuous, as I have argued, when it was surrounded by music and tones. (This is not to mention the living context of production, which was probably public, and so, like a play, introduced the living scene of life into itself as an ingredient of the esthetic experience.)

Such a picture, furthermore, has acquired some of the idiosyncratic features that make an individual. The Archilochos whom Archilochos writes into his poetry, as far as we have considered it, is a complex man. There is a strong military-poetic attitude at the center of what remains. We see here the attitude in fragment 1, for instance, where the War God and Muses are cited as twin patrons, and again in fragment 2, which praises the life of the spear in neat, almost effete, lines. So smooth, even swaggering, is the attitude, that flipness hardly surprises us, as it does in fragment 6, which talks about the lost shield. From fragments 1 and 2 we had supposed Archilochos to be a tough and competent soldier, but no idealist; he sounded like a man who could say "to hell with it." But wasn't there something shrill about the way he said the words in making this world-historical utterance? Probably not.

War was a serious matter for him, and he resented its cruelties. He hated the war lords of Euboea (fragment 3). He hated himself as a murderer, that is, as a soldier (fragment 59). He was, in fact, easily unbalanced from his sense of personal well-being: unbalanced by a sense of strangeness and numinousness in nature. Even more, it seems, he was unbalanced by a countering of his own erotic need, by the brutal rupture of his marriage plans. There are many Stoic poems, cautious and prudent, in which Archilochos tells himself that it all comes out the same in the end. And in the direction of sensuous hypersensitivity, and of vulnerability to the world, there are also rich and full testimonies to the character of his longing (fragments 84, 78), to the delight of an untroubled eye (fragments 29, 17), to the pleasures of speech almost for its own sake (fragment 17). At the other end of the spectrum, near the other kind of vulnerability to ideas, Archilochos proves himself a Stoic reaching out for a much more than soldierly consolation. He touches metaphysics with a deftness we could just barely expect from the man who threw his shield to the Saians.

The purpose of the present chapter is to bring in some of the many remaining fragments of Archilochos, in order, as far as possible, to complete the present portrait.

I *Poems of Sarcasm*

Many of the remaining fragments are small or so hopelessly cut off from their contexts that they cannot be discussed properly; they deserve to be left in their semi-articulate peace. But the poems which bear analysis confirm, and in some ways sharpen, my character sketch of the Archilochos who is to be found in his poems.

There is very little more of what I described above as a swaggering pose, or the pose of the casual poet-soldier. In discussing prosody, I have already referred to the first couplet, in which Archilochos calls himself the servant of the War God and the Muses. The brisk perspective of this piece affiliates itself with the kind of brisk Stoicism whiffed here:

> Nothing will I improve by weeping or make
> the worse by rejoicing and kicking my heels. (Fr. 13)

Why do such expressions seem to speak out from Archilochos' core persona? Perhaps it is that the confidence of his prosody, which catches its sentiments in seemingly unchangeable phrase, makes confidence and energy seem to be the chief attitude translated there.

The remaining fragments include those in which Archilochos most turns from casual virility, and *virtù*, to openly expressed pugnacity. We come on some of those poems, so famous in antiquity, from which Archilochos derived his main reputation as a sarcastic reviler, as a man who worked in iambs so harsh that they drove Lykambes and his family to commit suicide. For prelude, I choose a line in which Archilochos takes his complaint to Zeus:

> Paternal Zeus, I shared no marriage then . . .   (Fr. 99)

Of the attack on Lykambes, the cause of this loss, only the following is left:

> Father Lykambes, what did you utter then?
> Who robbed you of the brains
> which you had once; you're now
> the city's lovely laughing stock.   (Fr. 94)

Even when we put this together with the other fragments, like the poem on the eclipse (fragment 74), which may have been gibes at Lykambes, we are left finding this stuff tame. Aristophanes or, for that matter, Theognis or Hipponax, season us to tougher attacks than we have in this poem. Was there enough in what is said above to make the victim commit suicide?

The iamb had been associated, before Archilochos, with personal assault. In early religious ceremonies for Demeter, hopping iambic dimeters, scurrilously directed at men present, alternated with sacred rites: a certain awefulness of the sacred seems, as it does in gargoyles, to have been preserved in this art form. Though by the time of Archilochos the form had probably been largely divorced from its religious context, yet the iamb, energetic and ready for a fight as it is by phonetic nature, was still surrounded by an aura. It acquired especially forceful meanings for the argument it conveyed. Lykambes may have felt that force. He may also, as a seventh-century Greek, inheritor of a world which was still in many ways epic-heroic, have had a strong sense of his own *timē* ("honor"), his worth in public estimation. To be called "the

city's lovely laughing stock" may have carved him through; especially if, when the poem was written, Archilochos had already
come into some part of the great fame he won during his life-
time.[1]

The assault on Lykambes gains some strength when we add to
the present fragment a famous and sadly butchered fragment on
the fox and the eagle. The story seems a close replica of one by
Aesop, who was probably a contemporary of Sappho, and whose
work on folk-oral sources was known to Archilochos. The basic
line of the tale in both Aesop and Archilochos concerns breach of
contract. An eagle and a fox have made a friendship pact. When
the fox has to leave his lair, however, the eagle flies down and
steals the cubs, takes them to its nest, and devours them. Returning, the fox is outraged, and even more enraged at his own help-
lessness. Finally, in the Aesopic version, a strong wind blows up,
knocks the eagle's young to the ground, and the fox devours them.
Friendship has been converted into double savagery. Archilochos'
fragment 95, quite plausibly the conclusion of his telling, reads
something like:

> a great oath you have broken, deny
> me salt and your table's company . . .   (Fr. 95)

It is tempting to assume that fragment 89, about the monkey
and the fox, continues the attack:

> I tell you a fable, Kerux's son,
> a herald's staff, a bitter message.
> A monkey wandered, far
> from all animals, alone
> on a set-apart field.
> Toward him advanced a wily fox,
> with a clever thought in his head.   (Fr. 89)

The "fox" presumably is Archilochos. His victim, a projected hope,
is the monkey, as comic a figure to the seventh century Greek as it
is to us.

Whatever the explanation for the presumed effectiveness of
these attacks on Lykambes, Archilochos seems to have been seri-

ous, or at least to have been posing seriously, in these poems of
bitter disappointment over lost love. (The distance between pose
and actual attitude grows infinitesimal at this point.)

Another line comes out of his longing for Neoboule and argues
the same involvement with Eros:

> But limbloosing longing, friend, subdues me.   (Fr. 85)

His hatred for Lykambes may have been so strong only because
his longing and desire for Neoboule had been so strong.

His capacity for hatred receives more general expression in the
following:

> One great thing I know,
> to answer him who hurts me with hardcutting blows.
> (Fr. 65)

But so does his gift for faithful friendship, above all for piety toward man:

> But one man warms another's heart,   (Fr. 36)

and, better:

> No noble thing to blame a dying man.   (Fr. 64)

Love, even in a larger sense, does not conquer all. But a sense of
the ultimate equality of all men translates itself into an understanding of what it is to be man.

Sensitivity to human relations, too, is kin to an intense awareness of nature, that other large form of "the other." Two sharp
little poems remain to say:

> Beseeching a sweet return through the waves
> of the foam-coiffed silver sea . . .   (Fr. 55)

The statement is plaintive. A "sweet return" through the "foam-
coiffed sea" apparently is nothing to be counted on. It was the
kind of occurrence Archilochos might pray for. The other fragment is bitter:

> Of fifty men the gentle Poseidon has left
> us Koiranon.   (Fr. 114)

Play and bitterness seem almost to meet. The internal rhyming, between the endings of the Greek words "men" and "Poseidon," joins with the playing, though bitterly playing spirit of the "gentle" Poseidon. We know from above how much suppressed feeling is likely to be latent in this gamey assault.

This sensitivity convenes naturally, of course, with the precautionary Stoicism: the self-protective movement seen earlier, and, in Archilochos, instinctively internalizing, self-disciplining. A single well-known piece will illustrate:

> Moneybag Gyges no interest to me
> not jealous of him, not jealous of
> works of the gods, not asking for splendor
> of rule; things far from my eyes.   (Fr. 25)

Gyges was a contemporary, it seems, and already proverbially famous not only for his wealth, but for that fascination with money for its own sake which made his *Weltanschauung* famous. Archilochos is not jealous. Why? Perhaps because he is too deeply aware, or one part of him is aware, that pleasures dependent on external conditions are precarious. An external world as threatened and kinetic as that which Archilochos allowed himself to endure, contained many quiet warnings that only what a man is can nourish him.

It is worth considering a last fragment in which Archilochos turns to God in a way distinctive of him and of early Greek experience. The poet seeks understanding more than peace.

> Glaukos, Leptines' son, a man
> has so much heart as Zeus
> provides him day by day,
> and for . . .   (Fr. 70)

Our spirit and courage are measured out to us by Zeus. The careful measuring out of the language says this too. Regular trochees capture the careful gravity of the argument. Archilochos makes us feel, while we are learning, that he has found a place in which to convert life-distress into life-understanding.

CHAPTER 6

Archilochos and Classical Antiquity

> *Stand and behold Archilochos that*
> *ancient poet*
> *Whose iambs and multifold fame*
> *have spread from the dawn*
> *to the setting sun.*
>
> THEOCRITUS, Epigram XXI

SOME foreign cultures are opaque to us; the Greek, among those cultures which are at all close to us, is probably the most opaque. We understand, of course, its general point of view. It assumes the importance of the human; more specifically, the value of effort in time, the clear distinctness between subject and object in knowing; the qualified concern with the possibility of overcoming time. Given such broad features, however, often surprisingly little remains for our understanding.

What the Greeks made well, what *was* significantly theirs, enjoyed great autonomy. Vases, iambs, temples, were well-made wholes so realized that they left no obvious blemish for critical feeling to wedge into; they left little room for our critical understanding, as distinct from our admiration or appreciation. It is almost impossible for us to discuss the best made of these creations.

A Homeric simile drawn from human relations may help to show us one kind of past into understanding the Hellenic path. We can imagine a man whose conversation, through its brilliance or perfect adequacy to himself, relegates our responses to astonishment; yet heard in dialogue, he is far more intelligible. So works of Greek culture, which are opaque to us through their self-completeness, may be better understood when they enter into dialogue. I mean, when they are criticized, or talked about by other Greeks. We may not only learn much about the Greeks, and about Archilochos, by reviewing the Greek attitude to that poet; but we may learn certain things about Archilochos which in any other way would be impenetrable to us.

I   *Early Critics of Archilochos*

The influence of Archilochos on the Greeks cannot be the title of this chapter, for the man followed through this book never influenced his fellow countrymen. He was a concern to them, a demanding block or mass in what to the later Greeks became their own literary history; but with a few exceptions, as far as I can see, he did not enter into and mold the writings of other authors.[1]

The first recorded comment on Archilochos, attributed to Heraclitus, runs as follows:

Heraclitus used to say that Homer deserves to be thrown out of the musical contests and to be whipped, and Archilochos too.[2]

I suspect that the attack on Homer, which comes to us in this passage without immediate context, is prompted by hatred of myth, by a metaphysician's impatience with narrative means of explaining what is. This argument was urgently strong among the first Milesians, who, in the western world, were just discovering the delights of knowing and discussing being. They were apostles of a new vision. But why did they attack Archilochos, whose lyric directness must have seemed to them much less mythical than Homer's language?

We are perhaps touching the quarrel between *mythos* and *logos,* the former an attempt to persuade through sense-presentation, the latter through discursive compulsion. By this argument, also familiar to the Milesians, Homer and Archilochos might have appeared equally objectionable. In that case, they would have appeared chiefly as examples of poem-makers. In their exemplary function they would remind us of the curious Greek custom of reference to Archilochos and Homer as though they were comparable and equally great poets.[3] The Greek assumption, in this instance, is one more indication of our distance from the Greek standpoint.

Or can one speculate that Heraclitus might have been angry at the immorality of Homer and Archilochos? Could this have been an early form of that moralistic attack which rages in Plato and which often recurs in the tradition of comment on Archilochos?

Such an interpretation is not out of the question, but it hardly suits the general thrust of Heraclitus. He was not, as far as we can tell from the fragments, an ethically pious author; his physics directly attacked the poetic theology of the epic world. He was a pioneer. It hardly seems that Heraclitus would have shared Plato's conservative sentiments.[4]

The second recorded critique, from Pindar, may follow the interpretation suggested above (though presumably only by accident):

> I must flee
> the furious bite of slanders.
> From far I have seen Archilochos,
> assailer himself, assailed
> and at loss from enmity,
> deep-bite language.[5]

The tenor of the poem and the wider context in Pindar suggest a broad intention, a desire to stand apart from the arena of confused human passions in order to maintain a certain proud proximity to the Olympian. Perhaps this attitude is closer to that of Heraclitus, and less idiosyncratically Pindaric than at first appears. Naturally, Pindar, prince of images and prosodic magician, is not speaking against poetry here; but he may be attacking what is too personal in poetry, that in it which achieves the opposite of abstract presentation. In Pindar, as in the Ionians, there is a drive towards essence. Compare the elemental passions of the Ionians, their metaphors of fire, air, water, with Pindar's love of water, metallic radiance, and pure deep hues. This drive may have made Archilochos seem petty to Pindar. (It is worth noting that none of these critics takes much interest in Archilochos' historical importance as the first lyricist, an importance which is of the highest meaning to us now.)

The third significant criticism of the work of Archilochos before 400 B.C. is ascribed to Critias the Sophist, politician during the Peloponnesian Wars and a figure in some of the Platonic dialogues. It reads:

Critias raises the objection, against Archilochos, that he was his own worst slanderer. "If," as he says, "Archilochos had not spread this opinion of himself among the Greeks, we would never have known that he was the son of Enipo, a slave woman, nor that he left Paros from poverty and indigence, and so went to Thasos, nor that upon arrival there he alienated himself from *those* people, making light of friend and foe." "Furthermore," he says, "we wouldn't even know that he was an adulterer, if we didn't have it from him, nor that he was unbridledly, even indecently, sensuous, and, worst of all, that he threw his shield away. Archilochos was no good testimony to himself, leaving that sort of slander and scuttlebutt behind him." Reproaches raised not by me, notice, but by Critias.[6]

Whatever the motive, the attack is related to those of Heraclitus and Pindar; the baseness of Archilochos is the target. The perspective is no longer that of metaphysics or of the noble in poetry. Baseness is charged on far less radical grounds and from the typically social Stoic position.

Critias seems to be saying that Archilochos projected a bad image of himself and that this was his weakness, society's judgment being the chief criterion of value in human negotiations. On the other hand, as with Heraclitus and Pindar, we cannot be sure. We know too little about Critias, and far too little about the context of this passage, which is here only quoted from another source. Critias may well have been criticizing this bad image because it was bad, rather than simply because it was poor image projection. In either case, the indictment is the same. Archilochos is accused of complicity with those lower human instincts for one aspect of which Pindar had attacked him, and for which, on a higher level of generality, where poetry became the realm of the sensuous, Heraclitus also attacked him.

The three criticisms gathered here are few but precious, for they are the only significant early evidences left to us on the matter. They may have been selected for us chiefly by time and chance, not by human plan. Such unintentioned factors restrict our body of classical literary criticism even more ruthlessly than they choose our classical literature. Yet there is a representative quality, to preserved classical criticism, which repeats itself; it almost seems to imply more than chance in its formation. The remarks in Pindar, Heraclitus, and Critias offer us that representative quality. They offer, to mention the obvious first, no close criticism, no criticism directed to literature as esthetic construction. It was a long time, apparently, before the Greeks learned to take that kind of explicit interest in literature. Aristotle had already begun to take such interest in the *Poetics*. In many places he considered the devices of the word-maker, tropes, inversions, aspects of logic in syntax, and at all times he remained concerned with such basic elements as character and plot. His *Rhetoric* proves his interest in the strategies of verbal persuasion. But none of this is literary criticism working out from the texts; or even, in the most general way, out from language. It is all prescriptive argument, glancing at texts en route toward conclusive and predetermined convictions about literature.

Not before Longinus' *On the Sublime* do we reach a more genuinely literary criticism. There details of expression are closely surveyed and authoritatively assessed; the magic of language is wrestled with. But the perspective remains deductive and rhetorical. We are still concerned with the bag of tricks available to the author in order to make his point, or to persuade. It is one of the puzzles of Greek literary culture that the power to create vastly outdistanced the power to discuss creations. This mystery may relate to its sister mystery: that the Hellenic literary sense of the fullness of personality and character never translated itself into anything like a systematic psychology. The very word for personality was lacking throughout all the great centuries.[7]

Longinus, however, is already far from Aristotle in approach to verbal criticism, and much farther from the three critics of Archilochos whom I have discussed. It would be too much to say that their concern is chiefly biographical. On the other hand, it is much too little to say that Heraclitus, Pindar, and Critias are not interested in verbal criticism. They strike in between in a way which deserves mention because it is representative of extant earlier Greek criticism. They concern themselves with the attitudes of Archilochos which realize themselves in his poetry.

II   *Later Classical Critics of Archilochos*

Among subsequent mention of Archilochos in Greek literature, most is still to be learned from the strangely offhand uses of his name. From these we see, as in offhand references today to Shakespeare as "bard," or to Shelley as "skylark" or "pure spirit," just how deeply Archilochos had insinuated himself into Greek feeling. A few of these fairly random pieces of evidence add up to something more than a fragmentary picture.

Plato gives us a little evidence, naming (*Ion* 531a) Homer, Hesiod, and Archilochos together as a naturally joined trio. We have seen above the readiness of Heraclitus to consider Homer and Archilochos together. Later references to Archilochos show a similar readiness of such marginal authors as Heracleides Ponticus and Antipater of Salonika. The former, a student of Plato, is credited with a work, *Concerning Homer and Archilochos;* while Aristotle, in a probably reliable catalogue of his own work, lists *Sayings of Archilochos, Euripides, and Choerilos,* a title in which our poet finds himself in new but still great company. He also appears a little later when Antipater of Salonika (around the time of Christ) concludes an epigram with:

> To Archilochos today let us drink, and to Homer
> the man. The mixing bowl sickens of drinkers of water.[8]

Two other references indicate, through indirection rather than through a recording of lists of names, how well known Archilochos was. The first example was verbal. By the time of New Comedy, during the age of Menander, a common expression, "you tread Archilochos," had developed. The idiom stressed Archilochos' own supposed roughness and was sufficiently current that we understand the poet's remarkable entrance into casual thought. The second example, roughly contemporaneous, is from Theophrastus' work on meteorology, *De Signis Tempestatum* ("On the Signs of Storms"), and refers to Archilochos' poem on the rising of storm and fear (above, p. 51). Theophrastus writes:

. . . if the oaks bear good fruit, often many storms come. If a vertical cloud stands over the peak of a mountain, it means a storm, for which reason Archilochos wrote:
> Glaukos behold, the heavy sea is shaken
> by waves and a vertical cloud stands
> straight at the summit of Gyrae;
> a signal of winter . . .[9]

True, science and poetry were considered closer by the Greeks than they are by us. The perceptions of the poet and of the natural scientist like Theophrastus were thought particularly close. But even in Greek terms the passage deserves attention. It suggests

Archilochos' peculiarly authoritative aura. Nothing less could have brought him and his passage into such context, which at this point seemingly showed no concern at all for poetry.

On the one hand, then, Archilochos is becoming a commonplace of speech and reference. On the other hand, a myth or exaggerated habit of reference about Archilochos is growing up through these centuries after the fifth. I mean the tale about Archilochos' cruelty, and his savage iambic assaults, a tale picking up part of the energy in the earlier critiques by Heraclitus, Pindar, and Critias, but extending them much farther in the direction of personal assault, even of gossip. (It is clear, ultimately, that the tradition of Greek criticism of Archilochos, like that of other Greek heroes, has few edifying moments. A big squabbling family seems to have been at work here.)

The move into harshness often passes through grotesquerie, a direction taken, we suppose, in a strange play by Diphilus, a contemporary of Menander. The play was called *Sappho*, and seems to have shown, "as lovers of Sappho, Archilochos and Hipponax," poets who lived a century apart and cannot possibly have shared a single year of life. (Characteristic Greek indifference to positive history is shown here, as A. von Blumenthal is right to say.) What can these three *characters* have done together in a single play? It was domestic comedy, if we are right in guessing from what we know of Diphilus, and probably verged on farce: the two male leads gnashing their iambic teeth, while Sappho watched the moon.

By the time of Callimachus the myth and its tone were hardening. Callimachus himself seems to have left us:

> His the dog's black bile
> and the sting of a wasp;
> from both, the poison of his tongue,[10]

and thereby to have opened floodgates of poetic eloquence on the sting and bile of Archilochos. Bad-biled and wasp-tongued, Archilochos was to float down this current of cultural history. He was to be ferried by a host of wordmen. The most famous was Horace, but the company is varied. Some warn about the descent of Archilochos into Hades. Julian the Egyptian, who lived under Justinian, addressed Cerberus:

> Now more than before observe the portals
> of mighty hell with your sleepless eyes, now hound,
> be guard. When Lykambes' moaning daughters arrive,
> cut off from the light, pursued
> by Archilochos' iambs,
> then will not every corpse take heel
> and depart from your bitter halls
> to escape the attack? [11]

This is a developed, and really astoundingly strong, statement, as far as any of our textual evidence indicates, and suggests what a long operation of mythologizing Archilochos had undergone by that time.

The imputation about his mistreatment of the daughters of Lykambes is picked up often, as in the assault by Gaetulius (at the time of Caligula):

> This is the seaside grave of Archilochos, the first
> to baptize a Muse with bitter venom and gall,
> make blood on peaceful Helikon.
> Lykambes mourns three daughters hanged . . .[12]

The end of the poem reveals the wasps sitting on Archilochos' gravestone, to which the poet adds, as a warning to the passerby, that he should tread lightly, not to avoid troubling the dead, but to avoid stirring the wasps. These commonplaces multiply rapidly.

The tradition of literary hostility to Archilochos persists, though it is continually expressed in terms that suggest underlying respect. Besides the hostility, we still find the use of the poet's name as one of the great poets, as a companion to Homer. Such habit of reference supports the impression that the hostility to Archilochos, expressed by Callimachus and others, had become a turn of phrase rather than a felt attitude. Certainly the hostility was no longer based on knowledge.

III *Changing Critical Attitudes*

A number of more penetrating, and even more interesting, critiques are being made around the later margins of this history. It has been suggested already in the epigraph from Theocritus cited at the beginning of this chapter that Archilochos was recognized as a poet of great value. Recognition of this value showed itself in the later literature in a new attitude, that of taking the poet seriously. The first example, from Dio Chrysostom, deserves to be quoted in full:

There have been only two poets with whom none of the earlier can reasonably be compared: Homer and Archilochos. Homer was master of almost everything, animals and plants and oceans and land and weapons and horses . . . but Archilochos took the opposite direction, that of reproach [to psegein], because, as I see it, he knew that men need this more, and his first object of attack is himself. Therefore he alone, both after his death and before his birth, received the greatest divine confirmation . . . which all shows that the person capable of assailing, in language, who can grasp and show up other people's faults in his writing, is better than those who are used to praising.[13]

This is already a distant perspective on to Archilochos. We are in the fourth century after Christ, and Archilochos is far in the past. He was even more distant for Chrysostom, in the use of the Greek language, than Bede is for us in the use of English. (This is one more evidence of the amazing conservatism of Greek, which had changed relatively little in those eleven centuries.) Distance seems to have favored good sense. The remark on Homer is fine, though not so unusual. But the understanding of Archilochos, even if still impressionistic and morally centered, is impressive. We have not heard, before, the good caution that Archilochos is as severe with himself as he is with others. Critias had remarked in a totally different spirit that Archilochos had given all the evidence against himself, evidence of nonheroism, of adultery, of blasphemy, of hatred. There is no trace of self-justification in his poetry. And Chrysostom mentions the usefulness of such critical poetry, thus lifting the argument to an important concern: the function of poetry in society. Archilochos is here understood, unusually we now know, as a moral critic.

One of the last echoes of ancient secular comment on Archilochos, this time from the Emperor Julian the Apostate, carries this perception farther. Because his point is potentially powerful, it also requires full hearing:

To Alcaeus and Archilochos of Paros the Muse was no longer given in order to turn their thoughts toward happiness and pleasure. Obliged as they both were to suffer in various ways, they used their Muse in this connection, making the different gifts of fate more endurable to themselves, by attacking men who had done them wrong.[14]

There is nothing in this passage to indicate that Archilochos had attacked himself foremost, but there is perhaps a cognate awareness of the kind of purity and relief which can be experienced in poetry. Dio realized that poetic self-attack provides poetry with a kind of reflexive dimension which raises poetic attack against others to a generally meaningful level. Attack is given meaning as commentary on the human situation. To Julian, Archilochos similarly seems to have found personal meaning through poetic assault. One senses, between the lines, that assault is not only psychologically gratifying as a kind of revenge but is an effort at equilibrium. It is as though by assaulting a hostile world, one were somehow enabled to reacquire ontological evenness with that world.

As a final example of this somewhat fresher kind of perspective on to Archilochos, we can glance at the last preserved ancient testimony on the matter, from Synesius' *De Insomnia* ("On Insomnia"):

. . . as Alcaeus and Archilochos, both of whom expended their poetic gifts on their private life. For that reason a record is preserved, for all times, of what they suffered and enjoyed. For they didn't just shoot the breeze or declaim emptily on outworn themes like the present generation, nor did they put their gifts to the service of other people, as did Homer and Stesichorus, who through their verses so increased the reputation of the race of heroes.[15]

This point includes the others. Somehow, Archilochos' fidelity to private experience was the source of his psychological achievements, of his verbal energy, of his engaging power of assault. Not that he was peculiarly realistic, even in prosody, where he tried to speak with a fully human voice, but that he hewed his awareness closer to the individuality of human experience than did his predecessors, and all but a few of his successors, in Greek literature. The remark of Synesius, in fact, seems to be what we had expected to hear long before in Greek assessments of Archilochos. We have had to wait until the early fifth century after Christ, over a millennium, to hear a Greek expatiate on the individual voice of

Archilochos. That voice, which would seem to us perhaps the distinctively important trait in the poet, was of no apparent concern to early Greek critics.

There is little evidence that the ancient Greeks were concerned with their own process of coming into self-awareness as a people. The historical viewpoints of men like Herodotus, Thucydides, or Polybius do not stop at phenomena but constantly pierce to the causes and patterns of human events. However, there is always some shallowness in their conception of the genetic. Causes are understood as prior events with effects, never really as pressures with textures through which the new is laboriously brought to birth. This weakness transfers itself *a fortiori* to literary criticism, in which, as the present chapter shows, the underside of the argument rarely interested the ancients. The sense of literature as problem or as density is almost totally lacking.

The examples of ancient criticism, seen here applied to Archilochos, suggest a series of other ancient critical interests: of interest, only implicitly critical, in the canon of the great poets, say of Archilochos and Homer paired; of interest in the moral dimension, as we saw it measured by Heraclitus, Pindar, and Critias; of merely topos-like or turn-of-phrase interest in the moral, as reflected in the verses about Archilochos' poetic savagery; finally, of interest in the general world-perspective of Archilochos, the poetic assaulter. There was no room for concern with Archilochos' poetry itself in purely (or even mainly) literary terms. To the ancient critic the maker of the poem seemed to stand directly and transparently behind the made work. Thus he occupied, or preoccupied, the field of critical vision.

IV   *The Indebtedness of Horace to Archilochos*

For examples of closer criticism we would have needed to look at created literature itself, in which the Greek writer, far more than the modern, carried on a dialogue of resonances with earlier works. We would have done much more with those passages, properly understandable only in the original, where nuance, even slighter than irony, shows the affiliation of a later writer to an earlier. We would have seen Alcaeus reflecting Archilochos' episode of the "lost shield"; Anacreon repeatedly, and slightly, imitating Archilochos; a line of Cratinus, the fifth-century comedian, parodying a line of Archilochos; Aristophanes, in the *Frogs*, pick-

ing up strong Archilochean resonances in a pair of iambic dimeters as they were recited during a country festival; Callimachus, in his *Aetia*, clearly taking off from verbal springboards
provided by Archilochos. Fortunately, we have a clearer and
firmer single example of all this in Horace, and we can turn to
him.[16]

First, Horace makes two open statements of indebtedness or
awareness. He is quite clear on the importance of Archilochos to
him, though he qualifies carefully by writing:

> . . . Parios ego primus iambos
> ostendi Latio, numeros animosque secutus
> Archilochi, non res et agentia verba Lycamben.

> (I first gave Parian
> iambs to Latium, followed the meters and mood
> of Archilochos, but not the matter and words
> that assailed Lycambes.)[17]

He goes on, even beyond the qualification in the last line, to as-
sure us that he did not hesitate to modify the character of Archilochos' poetry (*mutare modos et carminis artem*, "to change the
modes and kind of his song"). Lest you consider me too servile, he
assures, remember that in my poetry:

> temperat Archilochi musam pede mascula Sappho,
> temperat Alcaeus, sed rebus et ordine dispar,
> nec socerum quaerit quem versibus oblinat atris,
> nec sponsae laqueum famoso carmine nectit.

> (Sappho tempers Archilochos with a steady meter,
> so does Alcaeus, though different in structure and meter,
> and seeks no father-in-law to slander with language
> and ties no noose of illustrious song for his bride . . .)

However, the strong first impression of debt to Archilochos clings.
Though the acknowledged debt is mainly technical, we know that
the best of Horace is itself, in large part, technique.[18]

The second passage, lodged in the middle of the *Ars Poetica*,
shows awareness of that technical ancestry while taking a bow
toward the Archilochean myth. Homer, says Horace, was the mas-

ter of meters appropriate to *res gestae regum,* ("great affairs of kings") and *ducumque tristia bella,* ("sad, huge wars of rulers"). But there is great dispute among grammarians about who was the first author of those later verses, *impariter junctis* ("of unequal lengths"), like the elegiac. The dispute continues, but one thing is certain in that early history:

> Archilochum proprio rabies armavit iambo;
> hunc socci cepere pedem grandesque cothurni,
> alternis aptum sermonibus et popularis
> vincentem strepitus et natum rebus agendis.[19]

> (Fury equipped Archilochos with his iambics:
> The foot slipped into the comic sock as neatly
> As into the tragic boot, so dramatists used it
> To make their dialogue heard, even over the noise
> The audience was making, the rhythm of purposeful action.)
>   (Translation by Palmer Bovie)

Anger lay behind Archilochos' own prosodic inventiveness, and the result of it, the iamb, was to flow into a long historical tradition, making much newness possible in poetry.

The presence of that influence in Horace's own poetry is far more often felt than provably active; yet it is felt so persistently that it drives even a major positivistic classicist like Eduard Fränkel to continuous heights of intuition. He refers to Leo's paper, *De Horatio et Archilocho,* in which the bond between those two poets was first clearly revealed, as having set much of Horatian scholarship on the right track.

Horace's elaborate use of iambs, in what scholarship has come to call the first, second, third, and fourth Archilochean meters, developed combinations of dactyl with iamb, reflects a medley of lyric experimentations once carried out by Archilochos. It is in fact simply the concern with mixing lines of different meter that most generally and most powerfully shows Horace's debt to the first known Greek lyric poet. Horace's book of epodes, reflecting his student experiences with Greek literature in Athens, is in that connection a decisive moment in Latin literature, showing it unsuspected prosodic possibilities.

More detailed echoes of Archilochos seem to be widely, though only half certainly, scattered here. Fränkel is a useful guide through such mysteries. Behind Epode XVI, Horace's harangue to the Roman people on the dangers of civil strife in 41 B.C., Archilochos is heard singing out his "Homeless fellow citizens, now grasp my words . . ." and assailing ignorance and public folly as Horace is, rather uncharacteristically, also doing. Behind Horace's *beatus ille* poem, Epode II, lies some deeply digested experience of Archilochos' Gyges poem with its similar protest against the mercenary life, yet also, we guess, some similarly urbane disclaimer tucked away in a surprise ending. Or, finally for our purposes, lines in Horace (Epode V) like

> At o deorum quidquid in caelo regit
> terras et humanum genus[20]
>
> (Whatever divine controls,
> in heaven,
> lands and the race of men . . .)

seem to recall Archilochean prayer parallels like

> Zeus, o Father Zeus,
> the strength of heaven is yours,
> you see what men do here
> misdeeds, impossible deeds.
> You notice the hybris of beasts . . .[21]

Yet no matter how far the last sentence, here uncompleted, is supposed to extend, we will not, in these Horatian reminiscences, be meeting literary criticism. Instead, we will find a subtle but not rationalized response to the understanding of an earlier poet. We cannot hope for much more. At this point, we simply touch the act in which the ancient critic was best able to meet his predecessors, the act of integration, a dense-textured reworking of the earlier text.

CHAPTER 7

Archilochos and Our Day

> With clear determination Archilochos grasps the first,
> the immediate, data of personal experience: the Now,
> the Here, and the I.
>
> FRÄNKEL, Dichtung und Philosophie

THERE may be good reasons, as this last point suggests, for the ineptitude and relative indifference of the Greeks to the explicit literary skills which we have come, especially in this century, to value highly. Of course in assessing the Greeks we must, first of all, allow for the dreariness dominant in the entire history of literary critical activity. Until our century, I believe, there has never been an extended period of high criticism. Our own advances are the consequence of a laborious historical preparation in which techniques of scholarship, earned respect for "art for art's sake," and fatigue with emotional or doctrinal criticism culminated in special fidelity to the esthetic structure. But we were separating ourselves off, in this activity, no more from the Greeks and Romans than from the rhetorical analyzers of *topoi* in the Middle Ages, from the hairsplitting Renaissance Aristotelians, or from the Romantic generalizers about the language of common men. The Greek literary theorists take a decent place in this company, especially when we consider what a peripheral thrust theirs was in the development of Greek literary culture.[1]

There is another way of looking at the relative indifference of the Greeks to critical skills, a reason suggested directly by survey of the ancient criticism of Archilochos. The Greeks were accustomed to another and far more direct kind of criticism than that which interests us; to criticism emerging from direct reworking of texts. Greek culture, much more than ours, was attuned to heard language, sensitive knowledge acquired through the ear. The printing press, and all that it signifies, has in this respect changed our sensibilities vastly, making us far more intellectual and abstract than the pre-Renaissance man.[2] The Greek poet, particularly among his people, was at any rate a specialist in the balancing of sounds and seems to have known all the meaningful sounds made by his predecessors. When Aristophanes wanted to mimic, attack, or merely recall Archilochos, he could do it deftly by inserting a wedge of dithyramb-like iambs into a choral ode. The tragic poets are forever carrying on this kind of dialogue among themselves. It constitutes—which is my point here—the most refined method of criticism which the Greeks ever made available to themselves. It is the way in which they were best able to say what they thought of their own literary history.

As far as explicit, rationalized literary criticism is concerned, Archilochos inspired little of this; by the nature of his poetic persona he collected around his work much that was most naively biographical, or philosophical-biographical, in the ancient critical manner. This continued to be so after the end of classical criticism and up to the threshold of our own moment. That is, it continued to be so to the extent that Archilochos in any way was experienced between the end of classical antiquity and our own century.

Already in later antiquity an ideological, and not a literary, interest in this poet was starting to make itself felt. It was something different from the moral judgments passed by Critias or Pindar, or from the protestations of shock in the later epigrammatists. Philostratus, in his *Lives of the Sophists*, says that the philosopher Hippodramus

was very enthusiastic about Archilochos, calling Homer the "voice of the Sophists," while Archilochos was their very breath . . .[3]

A mysterious assertion, unless it was intended to suggest Archilochos' aggressive, untraditional freedom of spirit. The passage looks forward to a harsher view, to that of certain Church Fathers who attacked precisely this open freedom of Archilochos.

Clement of Alexandria, in his *Stromata* (late second century), includes Archilochos among a group of reproachable "ancients." He asks:

. . . then must we permit Theopompus and Timaeus to write fables [*mythous*] and blasphemies: must we allow Epicurus, founder of atheism, and Hipponax and Archilochos to continue writing shamelessly;

while we hinder the writer who proclaims the truth, from leaving his useful message to men of later ages? [4]

Archilochos is accused of writing *aischrōs,* or "without a sense of honor." It is easy for us to see how much interpretation had gone into this accusation. Eusebius writes similarly, but more fully, in his *Praeparatio evangelica* ("Evangelical Preparation").

During the earlier Christian centuries, ideological interest in Archilochos is largely confined to observations like these. After such critics, and after those late ancient critics like Julian and Synesius sampled in the previous chapter, little more is heard about Archilochos for some centuries. (Or little more is heard by us, at any rate, though we can never be sure what languid literary perceptions may have crossed the minds of copying monks as the sunrays filtered in through their scriptorium windows.)

Texts of Archilochos in the Higher Middle Ages must have been hard to find. A scholiast of the period makes this observation, on being unable to find exact references to the poet:

the proverb is this: "Not even Heracles against two"; but what Archilochos' statement really is, we don't know; perhaps it might be this very one. [5]

In the tenth century Constantine of Rhodes prides himself, in the words of Ferdinand Lasserre,

on knowing Archilochos, but in fact cannot remember more than a few quotations from him drawn directly from lexicons. [6]

Similar pretensions, it seems, find themselves in a couple of thirteenth century Byzantine scholars, Michael Psellus and Nicetas Choniates, whose claims to expertise in the matter have long been exploded. As Lasserre again puts it:

As for the pompous assertions of Nicetas Choniates and Psellus, who are supposed to have commented on Archilochos in their literary lectures, their assertions no longer fool anybody. [7]

Archilochos next surfaces, importantly, in the huge re-engagement with antiquity which we call the Renaissance. He owes the beginning of his new life to Henri Estienne, the great, the indefatigable, imaginative, and scholarly sixteenth century printer. Estienne's *Carminum Poetarum novem . . . fragmenta* ("Fragments of Nine Poets' Songs") was published in Paris in 1560. It brought the early Greek lyric poets with it. This edition of Archilochos was not superseded until the appearance of Richard Brunck's *Analecta veterum Poetarum Graecorum* ("Selections of Ancient Greek Poets"), Strasbourg, 1785. By that time, Archilochos was a possession of the age of scholarship.

I *Twentieth Century Critics*

Closer to our time, his work becomes again the kind of intensely demanding document which, we sense, it was to many ancient poets. The ages of scholarship, we have seen, brought him back to the learned eye; but more than eyes, whole persons were soon to meet him.

It will suit our purpose to consider the contribution made by some of these whole, and in this case twentieth-century, persons to the reviving experience of Archilochos. Doing so, we will be learning more about the tradition of understanding of the poet, and at the same time practising for a final assessment of what Archilochos can mean to all of us, existentially, presently, virtually outside time.

All these scholars were tending toward such an encounter, at least in the sense that they were committing themselves to a faith; the faith that Greek antiquity had, in fact, once existed, and that we must therefore meet it from the center of our own existence.

It is on the surface remarkable that almost all of these significantly committed scholars of Archilochos were (or are) German. But it is only surprising on the surface. Werner Jaeger, Hermann Fränkel, Bruno Snell, Emil Staiger, and Max Treu have all been trained in a German philological tradition, which, at its best, sinks its deepest roots among the great German Hellenists of the eighteenth century, in Winckelmann, Schiller, Herder, Goethe. That tradition makes itself felt still today in the distinguished, humane scholarship of a Wolfgang Schadewaldt or Bernhard Schweitzer, and it did so far more generally early in this century. The faith in man, the complex but wholehearted humanism of eighteenth-century German Hellenism, made itself deeply realized among all the scholars listed here.

The relevant works of Jaeger, Snell, and Fränkel constitute a somehow internally coherent group of contributions. Snell's best work on Archilochos is found in his article "The Rise of the Individual in the Early Greek Lyric," published (in German) in 1941 in *Antike und Abenland*. But the argument, especially the kind of argument found there, makes large sense only in terms of Snell's perspective onto Greek culture in general; that is, only in the context of *The Discovery of the Mind,* the large and imaginative collection of essays in which our present piece is reprinted. The even more ambitious and more systematic studies of Archilochos by Jaeger and Fränkel surround Snell's book chronologically. Jaeger discussed Archilochos in *Paideia* (first edition, 1934), at the point where the book's argument shifted from the epic to the individual lyric world. The whole thrust of that huge treatise must be somewhat understood before the analysis of Archilochos is clear. The same is true in the case of Fränkel's *Dichtung und Philosophie des frühen Griechentums,* ("Poetry and Philosophy of Early Hellenism"), published in 1950.

It would be wrong to suppose, among three so different works, closer interrelations than those I suggested when I mentioned the humanistic tradition of such scholars. Each of these scholars, well equipped though he is with the weapons of classical inquiry, comes upon a hugely (and somehow demandingly) living picture of Archilochos. I have the inescapable feeling from these three works that Archilochos has here, probably for the first time since he wrote, been adequately encountered by criticism.

In each man's work humanism is made viable, and preserved from the sentimentality which usually corrupts it, by being incorporated into a larger cultural-historical perspective through which human events are understood as parts of an organic process; understood both horizontally in their own time and vertically in their temporal sequence. These three bodies of work stand in a tradition of systematic insight into the unity of the classical world, a tradition deeply impelled already by men like Giambattista Vico and Johann Winckelmann, and brought triumphantly through the nineteenth century by scholars like Fustel de Coulanges and Erwin Rohde.

Many of Snell's best insights have been inspired by an awareness of linguistic growth. (He is a professional and learned student of the history of language.) In his finest classical essay,

"Homer's View of Man" (1939), he examines the ways in which Homer's view of reality was defined by the ways in which he was able to talk about reality.[8] The most telling examples concern Homer's words for *ways of seeing* and for *describing the body*. In each case the points were similar; that in such descriptions details prevailed over general grasp; that this was so because the level of experience was still limited by the concrete forms of experience. "To see," an act normally expressible in fifth-century Greek in only two or three ways, was commonly expressed by nine verbs in Homeric Greek, verbs whose meaning ranged through the niceties of "to have a particular look in one's eyes," "to look about inquisitively," "to look with one's mouth wide open," "to be a spectator."

It is not that any of these meanings were excluded in the fifth century; only that few of them were used, and the others rarely; and that the general word *horao* had, for most purposes, absorbed the more precise words. The spiritual laboring from specific to general is also shown in the long process by which a notion of personality was worked on, though never finally achieved, in the Greek language. Stated briefly, the Homeric mind conceives readily of the *different parts* of the personality, from the specific organs to the more general notions of *psyche* ("soul"), *thymos* ("spirit," "anger"), or *noos* ("seat of intelligence"). However, it has no success in appreciating or naming the idea of personality itself, and little in understanding what *psyche*, as a single, unifying, kinetic principle, might be. Ultimately, as Snell is helped by this last material to see, Homer had little specifically linguistic perception of quality. It seems suddenly of the highest importance that in Homer one thinks "much" or of "many things," but not "deeply." Or even, by extension, that inner conflict is described by Homer in terms of formal debate, rather than of qualitative tensions. Interior agony can be shown, but not described.

II *Archilochos as a Modern Man*

It remained, as textbook language goes, for a student of Snell to carry this linguistic analysis into the center of the lyric age, thus to suggest at close range some of the distinctive characteristics of that new age. In Max Treu's *Von Homer zur Lyrik* ("From Homer to the Lyric" [1955]) Archilochos is repeatedly mentioned, each time as object of useful *aperçus*. A couple of luminous pages on Archilochos show how much is still worth doing in the effort to

acquire a fresh viewpoint onto the breakdown of the Greek epic
world and the emergence of a new sensibility.

Treu presses further with the question of quality, which he sees
in "a pronounced feeling for spatial depths, spatial thicknesses
and outlines" (*"räumliche Tiefe, räumliche Dichte und Profi-
lierung . . ."*). He finds this expressed in the totally un-Homeric
"vertical cloud stands straight" in Archilochos' comparison of the
island of Thasos to "an ass's spine," or in the shading of hair,
which we have seen in:

> She held a branch of myrtle and
> flowering rose and down her back
> and shoulders flowed shadowing hair.

Connected to this, among other awarenesses, is a new tactile
feeling, what Hermann Fränkel calls *Hautsinn* ("flesh-sense").
One form of it is *pathologische Anschauung* ("pathological perception"), a sense (erotically or neurotically colored) of the curious mood emitted by tactile awareness, as in "transfixed, clear
through the bones" and in "love that has twisted its way beneath
my heartstrings." Such perceptions are part of another new understanding: that surfaces seen are not merely surfaces, and, by extension, that virtue (or meaning, or value) may lurk where it appears not to be. An example of such perception is found in the
soldier who is tough, short, stout, without heroic attributes, without being towering, cleanshaven, or swaggering. Treu, like Snell,
readies us linguistically for a new grasp of the lyric ethic.

Snell's contribution, in fact, is decisive for the whole new tradition of insights which Jaeger and Fränkel have inaugurated. Snell
himself continued out some distance from these linguistic points.
Above all, he noticed the "despair of love" creeping, for the first
time in western literature, into the poetry of Archilochos (and
Sappho). He discussed the way in which a *sense of justice*, in
Archilochos, emerges simply as an extension of his personal will.
All this probes, but it is subservient to the main, bold, discovery:
that Archilochos, like the lyric poets generally, stands much more
nakedly than Homer before the perceivable and interpretable
world. In that sense, more than in any other, Archilochos is the
first modern man.[9]

Jaeger, as much as Snell, is influenced by Archilochos in the
process of discussing him, which is only to say that Jaeger takes

the poet seriously, accepting the existential demand ready to spring from the poet's works.

Jaeger's enormous work, *Paideia* (1934–47), examines the Greek conception of education in the widest sense; in reality it examines the conception of culture. Within the development of that conception Archilochos "speaks for a freer world" (Vol. I, p. 117), as Jaeger shows again and again.

Yet his meeting with Archilochos acquires its greatest meaning at another point. The originality of Archilochos is obvious, even if not easy to show, even if its obviousness needs to be understood, as it was by Snell, through all the trained resources of philology. We moderns have at least a first, a very easy and probably very accurate, sense that Archilochos belongs to our world. What we need, as students of the matter, is some sense of the traditional atmosphere in which Archilochos' revolution is taking place. Jaeger is at his best in suggesting this involved sense.

He is eloquent about the religious origins and spirit of the lampoon; the kind of bond, between obscenity and assault, and belief, which seems to reveal itself in many early cultural stages, and to have been conspicuous in Greece. The free play of aggression in Demeter and Dionysus festivals (in both of which Archilochos says he took part) has its later parallels in the Fastnachtspiele, Narrensprünge, and other ritual spring releases of western Europe. Without forgetting that Archilochos was a poet, Jaeger reminds us of the special character of Archilochos' poetic milieu.

At his best he brings this perception to the nature of subjectivity in Archilochos, and in Greek lyric poetry generally. It might have seemed, from the work done by Snell, Fränkel, or Bowra, that the Greek lyric was the product of relatively untended emotional expression. These scholars did not say it that way; indeed they were, I suppose, careful not to discuss the Greek lyric as Romantic lyric. Nevertheless, their collective emphasis on Greek lyric individuality, as when they wrote of the Lyric Age, had seemed to point in that direction; had seemed to stress the *revolutionären Bruch* from the old world, the break which Fränkel names and assesses with such skill.

But Jaeger takes pains to put this point fully:

Although the Greek poet, in exploring the new world of individuality, expresses ideas and emotions which are truly personal, he is still some-

how bound by universal standards, and recognizes the law which rules
his fellow men. . . . Certainly it [the Greek notion of "individuality"]
was not the Christian ideal of personality, by which every soul feels its
own individual value. . . . Greek expressions of personal emotion
and thought have nothing purely and exclusively subjective in them:
it might rather be said that a poet like Archilochos has learnt how to
express in his own personality the whole objective world and its laws,
to represent them in himself . . .[10]

This is a difficult and profound series of notes, worth extended
quotation because of their uniquely probing contribution to an
understanding of the early Greek experience. Do they fit Archilochos?

Earlier I contrasted the tangibility of things, as felt in poems by
Wallace Stevens and Marianne Moore, with something far more
perspicuous in Archilochos' depiction of the external world. Even
though that external world existed for Archilochos, it existed as
diaphanously as the girl with the myrtle-sprig in her hand. (Treu's
discussions of *Hautsinn* and *Räumlichkeit* in Archilochos help to
qualify and deepen this interpretation, but they do not make Archilochos' perceived world into a modern world of "trumpet vine,
/ fox-glove, giant snap-dragon, a salpiglossis that has / spots and
stripes . . .") Similarly, preserving the same, rather imprecise,
vocabulary, we might say that Archilochos' revelations of himself
in his poetry lack the sense of self, lack anything corresponding to
the tangibility of the outer world. The uniqueness of feelings is
absent in:

How I wish I could touch Neoboule's hand

or

I'm still alive thank god; to hell
with the shield; I'll find me a better one soon . . .

or

Wretchedly I lie desiring,
Soulless, with an anguish from the gods
Transfixed, clear through the bones,

where we feel in touch with what Treu called *pathologische An-schauung* ("pathological perception"), and where the intimacy of personal presence is intense. In each of these examples the generally human seems somehow to have embodied itself. There is of course no trace of symbolic technique, in the modern sense; simply, perhaps, a full realization of the generally human powers of response. It may replace much analysis here to contrast these lines of Archilochos with Dante's lament, in the *Vita Nuova:*

> Alas! By influence of many sighs
> Born of the thoughts that are within my heart,
> The eyes are overcome and have no strength
> To gaze at anyone who looks at them.
> They have become what seems like twin desires,
> The one to weep, the other to show pain,
> And many times they mourn so much that love
> Encircles them with martyrdom's red crown.
> These meditations and the sighs I breathe
> Become so torturing with the heart
> That love, who dwells there, faints, it pains him so;
> For they have on themselves, these grieving ones,
> The sweet name of my lady superscribed,
> And many words relating to her death.[11]

The point of meeting between Fränkel and Archilochos forms perhaps the most meaningful node in the growth of the re-experience of Archilochos. (Although Snell's encounter, rooted as it is in a growing branch of science, linguistics, may prove the most fertile in positive learning.)

At certain points Fränkel picks up, clarifies, and adds nuances to suggestions made already by Snell or Jaeger. Such continuations are worth mentioning here, partly because they show the self-confirmation of an imposing new tradition of understanding Archilochos. Building out from Snell, or from Treu, into the concern with surface and depth, Fränkel observes that in Archilochos

there is no "discrete" politeness, no mild toning down, no play of half-lights: absolutely lacking is any depth from the background. Everything plays itself off under the same intense light on one and the same level.[12]

The point, of course, is not the same as that made by Snell, or Treu, on the question of Archilochean surface; or rather the points do not meet squarely, though in dialectic they can be induced to reinforce each other. What matters is that a habit of useful concern has been achieved. With similar obliquity, Fränkel picks up Jaeger's qualifications about the individualism of Archilochos. He claims that Archilochos' subjectivity does not reveal

an individually formed and colored life picture [*Lebensbild*] . . . [but] what Archilochos communicates is in essence typical.[13]

Or, a little later,

The judging I [*das urteilende Ich*] in archaic literature is always intended representatively.[14]

The angle of perspective is different, and the directions of continuation numerous.

The distinctive awareness of Fränkel, into Archilochos' world of experience, concerns that poet's relation to his world. With these words, Fränkel launches a profound inquiry into that relation. First, he cites Archilochos'

> The fox knows many tricks, the hedgehog one great
>   trick—one great trick know I:
> to pay back with double interest
> the wrong another does me . . .   (Fr. 65, 118)

then adds that

Through this bizarre but drastic image of the hedgehog the I, the first person pronoun, establishes itself—for the first time in European literature—as the opposite pole of the Not-I, the other.[15]

We suddenly realize how bored we had grown with all the old talk about the new individualism of the lyric age. Or rather, we had wanted to continue considering the matter, but in terms, finally, that explored what it meant to be a representative of that new individualism. One thing meant was a new relation of subject to object, a defining of subject in terms of object. Perceptions of nature as well as awarenesses of personal differences, as in this poem, equally show the new clarity of Archilochos' perceptual world. Hatred, love, or simply the perspicuousness of a perceived island or girl all illustrate this point. Homer's world was certainly not indistinct or unclear. It shares much clarity with the Archilochean vision. But the direction of personal address or of perception which justifies Fränkel's use of the notion of polarity is lacking in Homer.

Fränkel develops another point, which is also concerned with the phenomenology of Archilochos' way of perception, and also drives toward a deeper account of what takes the place of the epic *Denkweise*. The crucial sentence, which crystallizes the argument, is this:

With clear determination Archilochos grasps the first, the immediate data of personal experience: the Now, the Here, and the I.[16]

Wars are experienced in terms of a lost shield; islands in terms of resemblance to ass-spines; generals of a certain kind in terms of idiosyncratic gait. The impinging personal impression leaves its mark on the poet. To a degree, it victimizes the poet, leading him through the vagaries of its occurrence. Yet only the poet, by his perceptual willingness, makes the occurrence possible. Only he is responsible for the existence of a Now, a Here, or even an I.

III *Contemporary Reappraisal of Archilochos*

Emil Staiger, one of the finest contemporary German literary critics and, perhaps not accidentally, a former professional student of classics, has for some time been working with the same perceptions that we see here in Fränkel. So had Benedetto Croce, long before his death; and so, in America, had Irving Babbitt, as early as his *New Laokoon,* which was concerned with the nature of the generic in literature. The thought, emergent here, will also help carry us toward a final confronting with Archilochos, toward the question of Archilochos and our day.

Staiger's *Grundbegriffe der Poetik* examines the three chief generic forms of literature: epic, lyric, drama. His great achievement, for our purpose, is to have isolated the peculiar relation of the lyric both to time and to effort. Drama, he believes, is full of tension toward the future; a sense of *the impending.* One feels that in every scene. Epic, on the other hand, is retrospective; it not only deals with material of a chronologically distant past, but its mood is that of recall and retrospection, of a survey of *res gestae*. The lyric, by contrast, is pure and immediate presence: what Theodor Vischer called

the instantaneous illumination of the world in the lyrical subject.[17]

The lyric demands attention for itself, in its presence. It reflects immediacy of production and presentation, conditions of it which Staiger illustrates but for which Croce, in his *Aesthetic*, has given an elaborate phenomenological account. That hyper-romantic account, stressing the identity of conception and expression, goes even further to make clear Staiger's main point: that the existence of the lyric poem is instantaneous. (This, however, only faintly helps us to reach that stranger and harder point, that the lyric has a way of existing outside of time altogether.)

Staiger's coordinate emphasis on the effortlessness of the lyric poet, thus also of his poem, completes the analysis. He makes his point especially well through analyzing Goethe's "Wanderers Nachtlied," in which, as he says:

It is not the case that here, on the one hand, is the *Abendstimmung* ["evening mood"], and there language with sounds at its disposal, which can be used on this particular object. But rather the evening, in and of itself, "sounds like language"; the poet accomplishes [*leistet*] nothing.[18]

The result is a product which shows *no* signs of force or stress. In this, lyric poetry contrasts sharply with "epic" and "dramatic," where effortless immediacy is no longer—and really need no longer be—the central awareness; where strategically planned organization of time is essential, and leaves its mark.

Fränkel had interested us in Archilochos' concern with the "immediate data of personal experience," and had thus taken us closer than either Snell or Jaeger—not to mention other scholars— to the essential originality of Archilochos. He had begun the suggestion that there was, in Archilochos, not simply a new relation to history but a new relation in history, a paradigmatically new stance, at least as far as man's esthetic experience goes. Now Staiger helps us further to see what might be radically original in this stance. He helps us to understand the deep sense in which the lyric poet is not manipulating time in his work.

Archilochos is very precisely not manipulating time. And by understanding this about him we acquire a key to understanding the peculiar meaning which he, as the first extant western lyric poet, acquires for us. In re-experiencing his work, as accurately and fully as we can, we reawaken in ourselves one of our own primal tropes of verbal achievement, as fellow members of the verbal tradition which constitutes world literature. It is not simply that we duplicate his effort, and that he was one of the first, if not the first, to make that effort. It is that in making that effort when he did, Archilochos the lyric poet "stood outside time," and to a degree simply met the world, as it was and is, at a burning but effortless middle-point: his own versed language. Where that language exists, incandesced to its nature, we literally continue to meet Archilochos as though no time separated him from us. And because he is our first-father, in this western achievement, we stand through him at the source of the western lyric.

APPENDIX

There are many historical cadres, in which it is worthwhile to appreciate Archilochos, which have not been appropriate to sketch in the foregoing text. In the following three essays I want to elaborate, on what I said about Archilochos, with some discussion of the inner character of the early Greek lyric.

A look at Hesiod's break from the world of Homeric epic will be a good point at which to begin. It will help to clarify some of the presuppositions of Archilochos' whole literary undertaking. In particular it will help to ready us for understanding the new subjectivity of the lyric world; it will do this more precisely than was appropriate to attempt earlier, in the body of this book.

From there I will go on to discuss Solon and Sappho, as representative lyric subjectivities, and as contemporaries of Archilochos. I will comment on each of these authors from a quite specific perspective: on Solon as a literary manipulator of his own subjectivity; on Sappho as a writer involved with "patterns of spiritual motion" in her poetry. I hope each of these perspectives will shed an indirect, but forceful, light on the texts of Archilochos.

The following essays have been previously published. The author is grateful to The American Philological Association and the Press of Case Western Reserve University for permission to reprint "Solon's Consciousness of Himself" (Vol. 89, 1958, pp. 301–11); to The Classical Association of the Middle West and South for permission to reprint "Sappho and Poetic Motion" (Vol. 61, 1965–66, pp. 259–62); and to *Symbolae Osloenses* for permission to reprint "Observations on the Conflict of Art and Didacticism in Hesiod" (Vol. 37, 1961, pp. 5–14).

Hesiod's Transitional Version of Epic Demand

*And I wish that I were not any part
of the fifth generation
of men, but had died before it came,
or been born afterward.*
[Works and Days]

HESIOD was born into a culture which was groping toward the conception of democratic individualism. It was breaking hard but painfully from the world in which Homer lived. The eighth century in Boeotia has been called a "middle age." Political responsibility was still in the hands of a landholding nobility, *basileis* Hesiod calls them. These men administered justice and fought wars. But at the same time there was increasingly effectual feeling among the peasantry and the nascent industrial classes that power should be distributed. Hesiod calls the nobles "gift-eaters," for instance, and in the *Works and Days* frequently alludes to the nobles' irresponsibility. But discontent with the nobility was not the only source of social ferment. There was at the same time a growing and widespread awareness of the importance of the single person. This situation can easily be read out of Hesiod's own text. He discusses the peasantry as though each member of it had a duty to his own soul, which outvalued his duty to political superiors. Justice is a principle which absolutely coerces the farmer, while society can only coerce him relatively. Hesiod's attempt to relate the daily life of common people to transcendent ethical principles—Dike, Themis, the order-pervaded world of Zeus—is the deepest unity between the *Works and Days* and the *Theogony*, his own two greatest works.

It is no surprise to find a strongly didactic and moralistic strain in Hesiod's poetry. Ethically centered cultures naturally impose

95

their basic concerns on contemporary writers: we think of Cato the Elder or Benjamin Franklin. It could be further expected that Hesiod, as an artist, would have had trouble reconciling art and didacticism. The *dulce* and the *utile* are not easily combined, especially when, as in the case of Hesiod, the inherited medium of expression is a highly refined, "artificial" verse-form. Hesiod had such difficulty, in fact, harmonizing art with morality, that he stumbles in the effort, and in stumbling shows his real nature and dilemma.

In working out that dilemma he takes us into an art-world which is far different from Homer's, yet which shares, with the older epic world, much of its distance and objectification. In a contrast, of epic with dramatic demands, we find Hesiod in the epic camp. We find him breaking from it to the degree he emerges as a person, in his work, to instruct the reader. But the result of that emergence, we find, is very different from what in Greek tragedy can be called "existential demand." It is more like, though still quite unlike, the personal demands made by the writers of Greek lyric.

After an invocation, the *Works and Days* opens with a picture of the two kinds of Eris, one of which drives men to evil, while the other encourages them to profitable competition. Perses is then urged to be industrious—to feel the spur of the good Eris— and to lead a simple, honest life, far from the bribe-hungry nobles. There follows the line (42):

> For the gods have hidden and keep hidden what
> could be men's livelihood.
> (Translations of Hesiod by
> Richmond Lattimore)

Then Hesiod breaks into three tales: of Prometheus and Pandora, of the five ages, and of the hawk and the nightingale. They are meant as commentaries on line 42, and occupy the next 180 lines.

These three tales are explanations of Zeus' refusal to make life easy for men. In different, and superficially contradictory, ways the tales show man's responsibility for the evil condition in which

Zeus has temporarily left him. The tales have a moral point. Yet they are not—perhaps with the exception of the third—"moralistic." They are aesthetically rich, and deal well with ideas through implication. In telling these stories, though, Hesiod faces a technical problem. Since the stories are thematically unrelated he needs to create verbal bridges into them, between them, and out of them. His manner of solving this problem interests me here.

The Prometheus myth opens (42–48):

> For the gods have hidden and keep hidden
> what could be men's livelihood.
> It could have been that easily
> in one day you could work out
> enough to keep you for a year,
> with no more working.
> Soon you could have hung up your steering oar
> in the smoke of the fireplace,
> and the work the oxen and patient mules do
> would be abolished,
> But Zeus in the anger of his heart hid it away
> because the devious-minded Prometheus had cheated him.

There are two surprises. There is a sudden transition, in the first line of the passage, and then again in the line starting "but Zeus . . . ," from the mundane to the transcendent world. In such flashes we grasp how close those two worlds were in Hesiod's mind. But there is a more typically Hesiodic surprise in the lines; the transition from direct address, aimed at Perses (43–46), to a third-person narrative style (47ff.). With line 47 the story begins. Such changes in direction or intention, in Hesiod's poetry, especially as a transition to or from a story, are frequent and meaningful. Sometimes they call the addressed person's attention to the story. Other times they enable the author to express his own opinion. It is worth looking at three further examples of comparable transitions, taken from the tales with which the *Works and Days* opens.

At the end of the Prometheus-Pandora tale Hesiod steps out of the role of narrating mythologist—"but the woman with her hands . . ." (94), "Hope was the only spirit that stayed there . . ." (96)—in order to describe present troubles, stating that "there are sicknesses that come to men by day, while in the night . . ." (102–3). Then we are back abruptly with the second person singular (106–7):

> Or if you will, I will outline it for you
> in a different story,
> Well and knowledgeably—store it up
> in your understanding— . . .

Perses' full attention is summoned.

After discussing the first four ages of the world Hesiod says that Zeus made a fifth generation. For the description of the earlier ages, Hesiod had restricted himself to an historical style in the third person. Suddenly he writes (174–75):

> And I wish that I were not any part
> of the fifth generation
> of men, but had died before it came,
> or been born afterward.

Then he goes on, as contemporary historian, to describe the iron age.

A final example of the point can be found at the end of the story of the iron age. The departure of Aidos and Nemesis has been apocalyptically prophesied (199–200). Then there follows (202):

> Now I will tell you a fable for the barons;
> they understand it.

This time it is the nobles, not Perses, who are addressed.

All of these examples illustrate a counterpoint between narrative mythical statement, projected at considerable aesthetic distance from the author, and abrupt personal intervention. We swing between the genuine epic and the nascent lyric world. The objectivity is briefly and sporadically punctured by the subject. The narrations, while presumably intended for Perses and the kings, actually speak to and presuppose a neutral, universal audience. On the other hand, Hesiod's interventions—practically interruptions of himself—are more or less directly thrust at Perses or the kings, and at the same time forge rather rough links in the development of the poetry. The narratives are full of implication, stories with meaning. They have intellectual content without bald declaration of ideas. But the interventions in various ways establish a moralistic attitude toward the enframed stories. They surround them with comment. At one time Hesiod will express his own attitude in these interventions; at another time he will urge Perses or the kings to watch out. In either case Hesiod's moralizing self is taking advantage of the necessary transitions in his narration, and punctuating them with admonitions.

This admonitory manner—which works from but slowly subverts the epic manner—also expresses itself on more general levels of Hesiod's poetry. The inhabitants of the transcendent world which frames the events of the *Theogony* are of three sorts: natural forces, like Chaos, Ocean, and Earth; the standard Olympian pantheon found in Homer; and what are generally considered abstractions, embodiments of ideas rather than personifications. In this last group I think, primarily, of the offspring of Night, whose genealogy is related in lines 214–32 of the *Theogony*. Those offspring include, among others, Death, Blame, Woe, Nemesis, Deceit, Age, Strife, Toil, Forgetfulness, Famine, Sorrow, Fightings, Battles, Murders, Manslaughters, Quarrels, Lying Words, Disputes, Lawlessness, Ruin. Some of these offspring—Deceit, Lawlessness, or Lying Words—are what we would call forces of Evil, that is moral corruption, while others— Age, Toil, or Sorrows—are familiar plagues of human existence.

Freidrich Solmsen has argued that these "deities" are original with Hesiod, and that it is puzzling that Hesiod includes them in his pantheon. They clash with the religious genius of Hellenism, which is hostile to abstract divinity, and anthropomorphic at its most characteristic. One explanation for Hesiod's inclusion could be that the existence of these gods was from his ethical viewpoint a necessity, even though aesthetically they may appear as little more than pale principles. Being a moralist, Hesiod saw reality first as a battleground of ethical principles. Not only was he aware of goodness—though he says little about it—but he saw and described the moral negation of life around him. He saw both moral corruption and the recurrent plagues of the human condition. And, as is evident in *Works and Days*, he considered the two things interrelated. In the story of Prometheus he observes that it was man's own evil—symbolized by the crime of the proud humanist—that was responsible for the creation of Pandora, and for the releasing of hardships and plagues into the world. Or, in the story of the flourishing of the just city and the ruin of the unjust one (WD, 225-37), it is clear that he considers the behavior of a society responsible for its happiness or misery. Evil and hardships seemed to him to be persistent and related features of human existence, and we assume that he deified them because they were transcendent features of reality. As a moralist, Hesiod was determined to make a place for evil and hardships, as well as for growing justice, in the structure of reality. He broke, as shaping poet, even through that veil of epic expression.

But the inclusion of evil forces in heaven is dangerous for a moralist, and Hesiod knew this. He leaves us, quite reasonably, with the possibility that if man could turn just all these principles would vanish from his pantheon, and another Golden Age would reappear on earth. The disastrous children of Night might disappear as, in effect, Ouranos and Kronos have disappeared from Hesiod's pantheon by the time Zeus begins his reign. They have an historical but not an ontological presence, at that time. Thus Hesiod does not put the children of Night into his genealogy solely because of a desire to account for all that exists. That is only part of his intention. Nor does he include them only to sing jeremiads over them, for after all they are divine, that is, they *are*, in the deepest sense. Rather, as a good moralist, Hesiod combines these motives. He wants to account for all phenomena that are right or wrong, ethically speaking, but he also wants to leave no doubt of his belief that wrong should and can last no longer than necessary.

Hesiod's grounds for including the children of Night in his genealogy of the gods are basically moralistic. Many other examples could be chosen to show his ethical bias following him directly into the making of genealogy. But none would have proven the point as well as the present example. It shows the determination of Hesiod to use the raw materials of Hellenic mythology, with its largely aesthetic character, as the foundation for an ethical argument. In other terms, it shows him viewing the epically objective from a subjective angle.

Turning from genealogy to story it is worth seeing how Hesiod deals with the core-story of the *Theogony*, the battle between

Zeus, with his allies the Hundred-handed Giants, and the Titans. This *Titanomachia* establishes Zeus' power permanently, and completes the series of revolutions in heaven which have disposed of Ouranos and Kronos. Once the Titans are defeated Zeus is free to create, and to raise, a family of forces of order—Dike, Eunomia, the Muses—and many others. The struggle with the Titans is a symbolic one in which Hesiod is telling how order entered the universe and how raw might was destroyed.

The problem he faced, in describing this extended battle (617–735), was to dramatize enlightened Zeus' victory, over the hostile Titans, with the help of assistants who were quite as savage as the Titans but who had joined Zeus. If he could have achieved that dramatization, Hesiod would have fused the vision of the artist and of the moralist.

However, the divinities in this drama have little personality. (So that we see here, again, how little dramatic this later epic work was). In their speeches Zeus and Kottos express similar sentiments, clustered about two ideas: that Zeus has rescued the Hundred-handed ones from bitter slavery, and that they must fight for him out of gratitude. All this time the Titans are simply undescribed, blind forces who join in the cataclysmic fight. They seem no more evil than the Hekatoncheires. We only feel their presence, but never see them. In fact, we entirely miss here Homer's gift for conjuring up the character of a god in a few words. Hesiod seems not even to envy that gift. Yet the fact is that he is dealing with anthropomorphic gods, which are denatured as soon as they are treated as forces or principles rather than as projections of human beings.

The actual battle which Hesiod described (654–725) is potent and authentic, one of his greatest visions. But its development has strangely little to do with its outcome. The battle rages, the thunder crashes, the seas roar, and great courage is shown on both sides: meanwhile no sense of victory or defeat is given. There is complete deadlock, apparently, up to the unusual expression, "the battle inclined," *eklinthe de mache* (711). We read (711–19):

> Then the battle turned; before that,
>   both sides attacking
> in the fury of their rage fought on

> through the strong encounters.
> But now the three, Kottos and Briareos and Gyes,
> insatiate of battle, stirred
> the grim fighting in the foremost,
> for from their powerful hands they volleyed
> three hundred boulders
> one after another, and their missile flight
> overwhelmed the Titans
> in darkness, and these they drove
> underneath the wide-wayed
> earth, and fastened them there
> in painful bondage, for now they
> had beaten the Titan gods *with their hands,*
> for all their high hearts.

Victory occurs suddenly, without our being given any sense of progressive conquest. (This is in contrast to the feeling of surging and retreating lines in Homer's battle descriptions.) Consequently, in this passage action and the course of moral meaning never coincide. They have to be plotted on different graphs. The main body of the fighting has no moral-dramatic quality, while the moral punch is reserved entirely for the last lines quoted.

There are two ways at least, then, in which Hesiod has failed to fuse aesthetic and moral vision in the *Titanomachia.* We had better not say that his moral speculation damages his art at this point. It is a question, rather, of lack of correspondence between aesthetic technique and moral notion. The *Titanomachia* has grandeur, and Hesiod makes his point. But he fails to take advantage of the resources of art, and such failure, for an artist, is serious. For an artist dealing in objective epic material it is especially serious. Hesiod is paying the price for occupying an uncertain position in the epic tradition.

It is worth dwelling on the deeper sense of the art-didacticism conflict, as we find it in the *Works and Days* and the *Theogony.* What was the source of that conflict? Did Hesiod's nature house two equally powerful, but warring, *personae?* Or was he so basically either a moralist or an artist that the presence of the opposite spirit—the aesthetic or the moral—was often difficult for him to absorb, and to harmonize? How are we to understand Hesiod's basic viewpoint?

Hesiod was basically a moralist. He was impatient with that in the epic tradition which most contented itself with an objectifying aesthetic surface. Surely he was discontented with much that was greatest in Homer. We can hardly doubt, thinking over the *Works and Days* and the *Theogony*, that the perspective is one of "right-and-wrong" more than of "beauty-and-ugliness." The avoiding of extended tales (the core of Homeric epic) and of personal confession (the core of the lyric creation) left Hesiod little room for wholehearted aesthetic efforts. At the same time the themes that he chose—the eventual evolution of righteousness in heaven, and the means to that evolution on earth—clearly inclined him to, and sprang from, a concern with the "moral." Still even here, sure as we feel of the basic quality of Hesiod's creation, a qualification is wanted. It can not be said that Hesiod was only incidentally an artist; that, for instance, he expressed himself in the hexameter only because he had no choice, was locked in one stage of a language's development. For he often wrote good poetry—as in much of the *Titanomachia*—and for the most part seems well at home in the hexameter. We reach the more intangible point that Hesiod's formulation of his ethic must have depended closely on his ability to articulate the Boeotian of his day, a dialect which bore at least a vital interrelation to his epic language. In other words, we cannot suppose that Hesiod's moral position developed from a linguistic or artistic vacuum. It was a position won initially from and through language.

What Hesiod wants to say—the residue of idea or message, to the extent that it can be isolated—frequently finds itself well joined to the way he says it. Content, in the sense of moral vision, is generally made one with form, in the sense of the manner of expressing that vision. But when a discrepancy appears in Hesiod's work, between content and form, the emphasis will be found to lie on the former—the moral point, as it usually turns out to be. That point will then appear—as is rare in Greek literature—in salient isolation. But the reverse situation does not occur. Hesiod never permits himself to be carried forward by style. Even in his love of the musical, especially of catalogues of musical names, care for completeness and piety wins out. To the extent that an authentic conflict enters the texture of Hesiod's work, disturbing that perfect balance of content and form toward which art strives, the conflict rises from a dominance of content over form. In literary historical terms that meant an uncomfortable dominance of the personal over that in the epic tradition which was most impersonal.

Solon's Consciousness of Himself

Solon is not deep or wise . . .
SOLON, fragment 33

IT hardly seems necessary to emphasize the point about Greek epic, in contrast to Greek tragedy, which emerges from the last essay; or to emphasize the bearing of all this on Archilochos. Essentially, epic "objectifies." This is the point with Homer, and one which makes his demands seem clearly different from those made by the tragedians. Homer's demand was for attention, more than for engagement. The tragedians entered lives differently. And in this general division Hesiod needed to be paired with Homer, and apart from the tragedians. The case of Hesiod was complex. He made "moral" demands; but he was also a persuader and charmer of the older objective world, dealing like Homer with material, mythical-moral material, toward which one should, as audience, be prepared to take a purely "objective" stance, feeling its independent qualities and coercions.

Greek tragedy and Greek epic, therefore, in some ways stand at a significant distance from one another. Tragedy makes a more intimate demand than epic. In relation to both these genres there are several perspectives in which Greek lyric (including Archilochos) could be considered.

It would be most expected, I suppose, that the lyric should be viewed in terms of a different kind of demand. This is in fact the chief interest I plan here to take in Greek lyric. But the notion of "demand," in this instance, should be rather particularly understood.

The lyric poet—whether in Athens or Chicago—imposes on us by forcing us to take an interest in his self. This distinguishes his work sharply from that of the ancient epic or dramatic writer, both of whom work out from themselves into public material, and into de-individualizing literary traditions. Yet the distinction of lyric from the other genres is not quite that sharp, especially where the ancient lyric voice is concerned.

The interest which Solon, Archilochos, and Sappho force us to take in them, as selves, is not quite the same as that demanded by Allen Ginsberg, Hart Crane, or even Walt Whitman. It is less an interest in personal uniqueness, though it is still an interest in what is self-centered and centripetal. With great ease, and no abstract intentions, Solon, Archilochos, and Sappho manage to let themselves and their perceptions speak into the generality of the human situation. This is what they require us to notice in the depths of themselves. The uniqueness of the individual is in them much less to be stressed than it would later be—and is in our time. Yet in the large picture *this* modern-ancient distinction is small. Solon and Sappho—unlike Homer and Sophocles—ask us above all to be interested in *them*. Naturally they demand this because their genres demand this. But genres are made by men, not vice versa. As they were, Solon, Archilochos, and Sappho could only write as they did.

The demand of Greek lyric, then, is on the whole different from that of the other two genres. It emerges from the personal demands exerted by the makers of Greek lyric. Here, three poems will illustrate (translations of Solon mine, unless otherwise indicated).

Solon is not deep or wise
For when the god gave noble gifts, he refused.
He cast his net on the catch, but,
Astonished, failed to draw in the yield,
Not equal to it in either heart or mind.
If I could rule, getting enormous wealth,
Governing Athens if only a single day,
I would willingly be flayed for a wineskin,
And see my race wiped out.   (Fr. 33)

Oúk ephú Soloń bathýphron oúde boúleeís anér
ésthla gár theoú didóntos aútos oúk edéxató;
péribalón d'agrań, agástheis oúk epéspasén megá
díktyoń, thymoú th'hamárte kaí phrenoń apósphaleís;
éthelón gar kén kratésas, ploúton, áphthonón labón
kaí tyránneusás Athénon moúnon hémerán mián,
áskos hýsteroń dedárthai kápitétriphthaí genós.

Even on first reading we notice the careful prosody of this fragment. The forceful, insistent trochees advance with considerable purely aural excitement, as in the sound repetitions of *bouleeis aner* or *hemeran mian*. The tetrameter lines are long enough for the poet to create an aural "atmosphere" carefully and progressively. From the outset Solon is skillful at involving us with the surface of his language. Historians have enjoyed slighting his poetry, preferring to consider him only a statesman. It is true that he wrote his laws in verse. But he wrote them well.

We are also impressed at once in these lines with the easy, uncontrived development of a verbal attitude. Such a calm assurance about the technique of developing a poem impresses us in most of the Greek lyric poets. Archilochos, Sappho, and Alcman all seem to be saying just what they mean to say, in just the way they mean to say it. Solon's poem, for instance, falls into two parts. In the first four lines we are given an attitude toward him. The first line is offered as plain, abrupt fact, though it shows fine aesthetic assurance, introducing the poem as a whole. The next three lines justify the first, by explaining how Solon was not *bathyphron* or *bouleeis*. The second line of the poem moves slightly out of the plain-statement mode of the first, speaking darkly of *esthla* and of God. In the following two lines we are carried all the way to metaphor. Solon has become a fisher, so astonished by the excellence of a catch that he fails to draw in his net. We do not know what "noble things" the god gave, or what the catch is, but we know, or are brought dramatically to feel, that Solon's lack of wit lay in being so dazed by some rare opportunity that he neglected to take advantage of it. The plain statement of the first line has been partially clarified, and put into a richer but at the same time vaguer context.

The next three lines form the conclusion of the poem. They begin with a shift to the first person and ostensibly explain, from that new angle, what Solon failed to take advantage of, though the narrator makes his explanation by telling what he would have done in Solon's place: that is, the lines are still a commentary, though in a different light, on the first line of the poem. (How much more fully commentary is integrated here, than in Hesiod). As a ruler (*kratesas*) the narrator would have had certain opportunities which Solon—we are to assume—also had, but ignored: the narrator could have become rich (*plouton aphthonon*

labon) and have been tyrant (*tyranneusas*). The poem is sealed
with a final line in which the narrator, the "I" of the poem, shows
obliquely just how much he would have given to have had the
opportunity which Solon missed. It is worth seeing that the exact
character of Solon's missed opportunity is kept interestingly vague
throughout the poem. This is mere artfulness, not concealment.
More important is the persistent recurrence, in different perspectives, of the theme set in the first line. The poem is strangely complex, yet simple and unified in mood. The "I" of the last three
lines is really just developing a single attitude in several ways.

The purely structural complexity of the poem shows itself to
be much more than that when one considers that Solon wrote it,
so that the critical narrator of the poem (who appears in *ethelon*
or *labon*) does not impersonate Solon's own attitude. (With another poet than Solon this last statement might be open to question. We might take the whole poem as self-ridicule. But this
would simply not be in the spirit of Solon.) The whole poem, in
fact, is the expression of an attitude toward Solon. That attitude,
of course, is critical. It tries to put Solon in an absurd light, im-
plying that he is stupid and hesitant. Yet the poem is finally not
self-ridicule, because the "I" in the poem very nicely discredits
himself. The last three lines prove that. The last line, in fact, is
such a violent expression of self-debasement, on the narrator's
part, that it turns the poem into an attack against the narrator
rather than an instrument of self-criticism on Solon's part. The
concealed attack is highly successful. Despite initial appearances
to the contrary, the poem becomes a subtle vehicle for Solon's
praise of himself on moral grounds.

Of particular interest, here, is the kind of self-consciousness
which Solon shows in the poem he has written. It is chiefly
through self-consciousness that he represents his inner life to us.
In itself his verbal accomplishment, in putting an attitude toward
himself into the mind of another, is significant. The development
and expansion of the notion of the self was a gradual and difficult
feat of early Greek experience. The attainment of self-consciousness required, for one thing, a realization within the individual
of the distinctness of his own self from the selves of his fellow-
citizens. It is that kind of realization which Solon attains artisti-
cally, by artificially standing outside of, and looking at, himself in
this poem. To integrate such self-awareness into art is difficult.

This is the place to open a qualification which holds generally for the Greek poets in their quest for the self. Those poets were not in search of an ineffable essence in themselves. Roughly speaking, they did not try to express the "soul," in the post-classical sense of the word. They looked on themselves as parts of the natural world, and took it for granted that their experiences and attitudes were expressible in natural and accessible language.

In the fragment considered above, Solon writes no *deep* awareness of his self: I stressed only his surprisingly "objective" perception of himself as a distinct entity among other selves. This kind of perception does not set him apart from other Greek lyric poets, but, on the whole, it is rarer with most than with Solon. Archilochos tells us a good deal about himself: what he loves, what he hates, how the sense-world strikes him. But in all this "expression of himself" he integrates little awareness of his own self's distinct nature and position. This is what limits his self-consciousness: his self has not yet been brought into a system of defining relations. When he writes that

> By spear is kneaded the bread I eat, by spear my Ismaric
> wine is won, which I drink, leaning upon my spear,
> > (Translations of Archilochos by
> > Richmond Lattimore)

we feel we are learning a lot about the poet, and it is clear that he has here raised the physiognomy of his nature into reason and form. Yet his statements emerge too directly *out of* the self to include any reflexive awareness of the self. This is generally true of Sappho and Alcman too.

With Solon the "outer" conditions for such reflectivity were more favorable than with these other poets. In his youth he was an *homme d'affaires* and traveled through Ionia, visiting in highly cultivated court circles. He was from a good family and knew the best men of Athens. More importantly, he had from the time of his youth an interest in politics, becoming in middle age archon of Athens, with exceptional powers. From this position he gave the Athenians new laws, new currency, and a new constitution. As archon he was continually called on to mediate between the aristocracy and the proletariat. This difficult life in the public eye, with the demands it made on his natural integrity and decency, no doubt forced him to a clearer awareness of himself, of his nature, and of his intellectual "position." Caught between cross-fires of opposing view-points he came to realize what he stood for, and therefore inevitably to have a better idea of what he was. In these circumstances, too, he can be contrasted with the majority of the remaining Greek lyric poets: Archilochos the soldier, Sappho the lover, Alcman the emancipated slave.

These "outer" conditions of Solon's self-awareness are certainly relevant here, for they are constantly integrated, as subjects as well as ingredients of attitudes, into his verse. I want to clarify this point by looking at three poems, starting with one of Solon's most famous elegies:

> To the common people I gave the strength they need,
> Neither retracting their honors nor tempting with more:
> Those who had power and position through wealth,
> Those too I was careful to shelter from indignity.
> I took my stance, casting a strong shield over both parties,
> And allowed neither to triumph unjustly.

Again we notice the confident and skillful prosody. Solon has made the poem into the naturalness of a calm mind. But especially interesting for the present question is the way the form echoes his viewpoint. The poem is divided into three "couplets," each of them closed, as generally in the Greek elegy. The first couplet coincides with Solon's statement of just how much he gave to "the people," while the second couplet does the same for the statement about the aristocracy. In each case the talk of limited giving is reinforced precisely by the formal limits of the poem. Just as the "idea" of the final couplet unifies the "ideas" of the first two couplets, so that last couplet appears as a kind of formal crown to the poem. The three distinct acts of Solon are marked off and "formalized" by the structure of the poem.

Solon's image, of "casting a strong shield over both parties," is successful and clear, provided it isn't followed into its sensuous details. Such following is not invited, because Solon's poetry is unusually non-sensuous, relying little, for example, on exact visual imagery. Thus we are ready to read such an image as this of the shield simply for its conceptual drift. That drift is clear. Solon saw himself as a strong, impartial leader, as he informs us in this poem, and as such he both unified—indeed, clamped down on—both factions of the city, and cast a symbol of protection, the shield, over both of them. In casting the shield, then, he tries to make it clear that he is not only a limit-prescriber for his society, but also its unifier and protector. The poem develops a surprisingly complex attitude of Solon toward himself. It is characteristic of his mind that no trace of "egotism" enters this attitude, no foolish or imprudent self-praise.

In another poem, written in iambic trimeters (fragments 36, 37), Solon expresses more dramatically this awareness of his self's political context. He relates the four good things he has done for Athens. He has freed the land from bondage (mortgages), has brought many Athenians back home, has freed many Athenians from slavery, and has given laws equally to the good and bad. In the fragment (37) which belongs to the end of that poem he says that if he had done what his opponents had wanted, the city would have lost many men. At the end we read:

> This was why I turned like a wolf in a dog pack
> Defending myself from attack on every side.

This time he has joined a clear, strong image to his forceful iambs, making a peculiarly final statement of his political troubles. In a way the visual objectivity, with which Solon here sees himself, reminds us of fragment 33. Sappho, expressing her love-consumed self, or Archilochos his passionate, brutal self, are rarely able to stand beyond those selves, and assess their own natures with this clear Solonian eye. Seldom is Solon, for that matter, able to translate his self-awareness into visual terms.

As a final example I want to mention a fragment (32) in which Solon's theme is his distinctively ethical self.

> If I spared my fatherland
> And did not seize hold of tyranny and force,
> Polluting and shaming thereby my reputation,
> I am not ashamed. For I think that thus
> All the more I excel other men.

The "I am not ashamed" is a potent understatement. It introduces, here, a direct statement of moral principle, in which Solon himself breaks out rather anti-poetically, from the surface of his verse, and addresses us with an unaccustomed edifying voice. (Just as he is never egotistic, he is almost never moralistic.) He is assessing his political achievement, and asserting the unity of moral behavior with right political action. He asserts this not as an easy gnomic idea, but as a comment on his own experience in the political world. Even in the case of the clause "all the more," it is important to see what a conquest over ordinary language and ordinary sentiment has been won. In Solon's case, it appears to be won precisely by his attention to his own nature and its experiences.

The evidence of Solon's self-awareness and self-presentation hardly goes farther than the few fragments assembled here. There are some 283 verses of Solon extant, and few of them concern the present question. I want to draw together a few observations suggested by the poems already discussed.

In his poetry, Solon did not seek for the self as an ineffable essence in him. In this he was like the other Greek lyric poets. In most of them "expression of self" is only a hesitant step taken toward the discovery of the "I." Such "expression" is different from "reflection onto the self." Solon is exceptional for his "reflectiveness" in this sense. Even in *his* poetry, though, we see chiefly a reflection onto the public characteristics of the self, a preoccupation which was to be expected from so publicly oriented a man. In the fragments considered here, Solon has been looking back (in time as well as in "space") on the events of his moral life: its decisions, actions, situations. He looks back as though from a great distance on these events, with an innate nobility of vision which Hermann Fränkel calls "unfeierlichen Pathos, das für seine Haltung und Dichtung bezeichnend ist." His self presents itself to him with none of the immediacy of its "accidents," such accidents as sense-impressions. Nor does it appear as a center of reason or aesthetic appreciation, although in its poetic incarnation it is translated aesthetically. His self emerges, through the language in which he presents it, as a generative core of his moral life. The moral argument in Hesiod was blurred, rejected far and obscuringly, as it turned out, into epic material. In Solon the moral argument emerges directly, as an immediate result of his negotiation with himself.

It remains to consider Solon's distinctive self-awareness briefly in relation to his whole (poetically expressed) vision of life. A single example will suggest that relation and indicate the literary-historical importance of Solon's self-consciousness. He is aware of his own self as a center of moral events. It is no surprise, then, to find that he looks on other selves as that too. He continues the tradition, first evident among the Greeks in Hesiod, of calling upon the individual to grow conscious of his moral responsibilities. We have seen Hesiod doing this in *Works and Days*, where, generalizing from his own experience with an unjust brother, he clearly insisted that Justice is a real principle, one which must be respected. Hesiod had spoken in universal terms, convinced that justice is an obligation falling equally on every man, king or peasant. Solon makes this same projection from his own experience, insisting on the absolute wrong of lawlessness and the absolute right of lawfulness. Both these principles, he claims, present themselves to every individual and cannot be sidestepped. His awareness of his moral self is clearly related to this insistence on the moral responsibility of every self.

This appeal to the individual conscience is made with great force in Solon's long poem *To the Athenians* (fragment 4). That poem opens with a diatribe against the injustice of the leading, insatiable citizens, and culminates in the broad charge that they neglect Justice. For this, Justice brings slavery and strife into the city.

> Thus public calamity comes to each man's home
> The gates of his courtyard are unwilling to guard him,
> Over the high gate calamity leaps, and finds him,
> Even though fleeing he waits in the innermost nook of his room.

The picture of the city haunted to its last nook by evil is one of the great visions of Greek poetry. This evil, which follows every man into his home, is the product of a discord in the state (*stasis*) which was caused by a few men. Individual evil, that is, can cause a flood of evil for a whole state. Solon emphasizes the moral responsibility of the individual in his community. In his elegy *To Himself* (fragment 13) he had emphasized the individual's responsibility to his descendants, or *genos*. Speaking of the man who is unjust-minded, he says:

> One man pays at once, another later. If
> The man himself escapes the fate of the gods,
> It comes most surely again; though blameless, the children
> Or later descendants will pay his penalty.

In one way or another, the individual's moral behavior extends far beyond himself. For that reason, Solon is saying, the individual needs to know his moral self. This insistence seems to be related to his own self-awareness. It might even be said that Solon's self-consciousness is the ground for his belief in the importance of self-awareness in others. Simply stating this relationship makes the importance of the context of Solon's self-awareness clear.

If Solon's distinctive form of self-consciousness is connected with his consciousness of the "situation" of the self in general, then self-consciousness becomes an ingredient in his *historical* achievement. That achievement was many-sided, of course: he was a creative law-giver, economic reformer, and politician—in the Greek sense—as well as a poet. Still there was unity to his efforts. It lay in the conviction of the worth of the individual self's moral development. I don't suppose that Solon admired Justice on abstract grounds. He admired it for its power to bring into the state a harmonious situation in which each man could find his place and direction for growth. The same motive, no doubt, urged Solon to free the land from slavery, that is from mortages which kept the majority of Athenians in debt, and therefore unable to develop with moral self-respect. For the same reason, I guess, Solon opened the Ecclesia to the Thetes, and the judicial courts to everyone. It is important, of course, not to consider the Solon of these acts a committed democrat. In many ways he valued the traditional organization of society; for instance, in his admiration for rightfully inherited wealth. Yet he was a democrat to the extent that democracy meant a collection of morally responsible, that is self-aware, individuals.

The consciousness of the importance of each moral self, on which Solon's historical achievement rests, may be related to his own self-consciousness. This point gives peculiar importance to the poetic fragments analyzed here. They permit us to see Solon dealing intimately with his own being, and in a manner unique among Greek lyric poets. His self-consciousness is distinctively moral and radiates a demand onto moral self-consciousness in other men. It shows how immediately demanding lyric poetry could make the ethical concerns which in epic were muted and in tragedy expressed through an entirely different, oblique and participatory, channelling of affects.

Sappho and Poetic Motion

Hither to me from Crete
to this holy temple
Where you will find your lovely
grove of apples,
And your altars perfumed with
frankincense.

SAPPHO, fragment 2

IT is possible to view the lyric as a fairly direct effort to "ob-
jectify" or "project" the inner life. But as is clear in the case of
Solon, such "projection" is only possible in terms of the rules of
language, and of one's introspective relation to himself. The lyric
demand may be far more immediate than the epic—Solon's than
Hesiod's—but it is only immediate in the way permitted by literature. (This applies to Archilochos in the same way as to Solon.)
Solon was not free, psychologically or metaphysically speaking, to
"pour himself forth" into his verse. But this was far truer of the
epic writers. Homer worked through and into a "subjectivity-
muting" tradition, as did Hesiod, despite his restlessness with the
epic stance. The question of rules of language, of linguistic limitations upon pure self-expression, is in all these writers no less
important than that of tradition-made psychological limitations:
ultimately the two questions are closely related. The rules of language, including not only the "laws" of grammar but the body of
tropes and verbal habits which constitute literary tradition, are
deeply involved with the laws or limitations on the inner life: the
inner life itself only developing and ripening in terms of language.
What must be projected is already unconsciously verbalized. Has
the lyric poet, then, any inward life, in some degree independent
of language, which he can project? How closely do language and
subjectivity, in this case, amount to the same thing? Answering
this, even in part, will help us to appreciate the ancient lyric de-

mand. It will bring us closer to Archilochos, even while we are not focussing on him.

I will content myself, in answer to the complex question, with the notion that in the lyric poet there are certain dramatic tendencies which seek expression in words. The points about Solon will thus be put in other terms. One form the lyric poet's dramatic tendencies adopt is that of motion—toward, away from, and of different kinds. There is a kind of inner kinesis in the psyche. What is important about this *kinesis*, what forms its *raison d'être*, is its power to dramatize certain attitudes, or constellations of feelings. Thus the inner drama of motion "upward" will often be associated with the notion (or attitude) of spiritual ascension, and that of motion "downward" with the notion of spiritual descent, corruption, and so on. It is obvious—but worth saying— that the association between such felt inner patterns of movement, and actual spiritual conditions, the "objectively" psychological, is purely imaginary. Such an association has no grounding in "physical" reality. Motion upward has nothing real to do with spirituality. Yet the kind of association involved here is a fact of the utmost importance both in ordinary language and in "literary" language. Here I look to the way Sappho, in her verse, manipulates a pair of these kinetic forces, thus exercising what for her was a characteristic inner demand.

Motion "toward" or "away from" the presenter of the poem is of continual importance in the largely fragmentary remains of Sappho. (As a theme in her poetry it occupies the place played, in Solon's poetry, by spiritual movement in toward the poet as subject.) This pattern has a fundamental connection with Sappho's erotic temperament, as we shall see later. First we can notice a single famous example of *stasis,* arrested motion, in her verse, and then work out from that point. In fragment 31 (1–4) we read

> Beyond all heavenly fortune seems to me
> the man who sits facing you and listens
> intimately to your sweet speech . . .
> (Translations of Sappho by P. M. Hill
> unless otherwise indicated)

The nearness of "the man" (*kenos*) to Sappho's beloved is doubly emphasized by the use of both "facing" (*enantios*) and "near" (*plasion*) to describe his location. The emphasis fits with the poet's double intention: to express jealousy of the "nearness" of "that man" to the beloved, and to contrast "the man's" presumed ability to endure such radiant presence, with Sappho's own debility in that presence. The man's "location," under the circumstances, is significant.

Sappho frequently links the amatory mood, founded by such a treatment of "location," with motion toward the presumed presenter of the poem. Often such motion is put into the form of a "conventional" supplication of divinity, usually of Aphrodite. (*Supposed* conventionality: after all the tradition was to call upon divinity or the Muse, as Homer did, to *speak*, not to approach.) Thus in fragment 1, addressing Aphrodite, Sappho says (5-7):

> But come to me, if ever in the past, at other times,
>   You hearkened to my songs,
>   And harnessed the golden chariot, and left
>   Your father's house and came to me.

It becomes clear in this poem that Sappho *really* wants the goddess to come, as the goddess has done before. Lines 9-13 are in fact devoted to fanciful but—in the poetic context—quite real former descents of Aphrodite to Sappho. A tangible sense is created here that the poet is inviting a real presence to come near her. This sense is reinforced by a return to the invitation at the end of the poem. Sappho says (25-26):

So come to me now, release me from grievous care . . . and, at the last (28):

> And be my ally.

Goddess stand by my side, the poet says.

In another poem (fragment 2) Sappho makes such an invitation—again also to Aphrodite—even more tangible. We are here far from the verbal world in which the poet simply wants "inspiration" from the Muse. The actual presence of Aphrodite, always in terms of literary illusion, is invited with a variety of sensuous details which makes the mood of approach and nearness unmistakable.

> Hither to me from Crete
> To this holy temple

Where you will find your lovely grove of apples,
And your altars perfumed with frankincense.
(My translation)

And she goes on with description of the water, branches, roses, leaves, which make a seductive bower of the place to which Aphrodite is being invited. The notion of seduction, in fact, is in place here. Particularly—or is this to confuse the "divine" with the human?—when we consider Sappho's own homosexuality, such an invitation to Aphrodite seems erotically tinged. At the end of the poem (13–16) it appears that Aphrodite is wanted chiefly to perfect some mood of festivity, where nectar is being drunk. But it is almost as though the goddess would *be* the perfection of that mood. She will be no mere Ganymede, trotting with her chalice from cup to cup.

Finally, to turn to an example of verbalized approach which exists on a more "objectified" plane, there is the description of the wedding of Hector and Andromache (fragment 44). Here the poet is not calling the wedding assembly *toward* her; she describes the movement of the newly married pair toward Troy, and their joyous reception in the city. Yet though the poem is badly mutilated it is still suffused with a strong sense of "arrival." While projecting the entire situation into unlocalized objectivity, Sappho has in feeling miraculously taken the place of a Trojan woman welcoming home her leader and his bride. As she describes the sound of cymbals, the holy songs sung, the smell of incense in the streets, we have a sense of being there, of witnessing the "coming." Characteristically of Sappho—though also part of the exigency of the subject—we are made almost insensibly aware of the place *toward which* motion is taking place, though much less aware of the motion itself.

Motion "away from" a set point is, by contrast, a less important dramatic theme in Sappho's verse. She easily conceives her language around the axis of departures and absences, but cannot so readily dramatize the feeling of "motion from" as of "motion toward." In fragment 1 a brief passage of great technical refinement shows both axes of Sappho's inner drama together, and introduces the point. Aphrodite is imagined as having asked Sappho, formerly, how she can help her to win over a recalcitrant lover. The goddess inquires (19–24):

> And whom must I now bend to your love—
> Who is it, Sappho, who has wronged you?
> For even if she flees you,
>   quickly will she pursue you,
> And if she now refuses gifts,
>   tomorrow she will give them;
> Yes, and if she loves you not to-day
>   soon will she love you, despite herself.

Concisely, Sappho expresses the whole dialectic of her inner life. Departure from and motion toward an established point—the poet herself—are both dramatized. The interaction of the poles is made peculiarly tight through the embodiment in a single person, Sappho's beloved, of both forms of motion. Now she is fleeing, tomorrow she will pursue.

In two of the other major fragments of Sappho we find the notion of parting clearly emphasized, and with it, though not explicitly described, a sense of "motion away" from the poet. Fragment 96 is addressed to Atthis, to console her for the loss of a girl who has gone to Lydia:

> . . . how especially she loved your singing.
> And now among the Lydian women she shines . . .

The bulk of the remaining poem is concerned with a simile, comparing the absent girl to the moon, which is pre-eminent among the stars and shines placidly down on the peaceful world. The force of the whole is to emphasize the beautiful *distance* of the absent girl. Only in the lines quoted above is her departure felt; the rest of the poem makes the loss tangible.

Fragment 94 presents a dialogue between Sappho and a friend who has left her:

> . . . she wept bitterly when she left me and said to me

is the introduction to the dialogue. Most of the remaining poem, then, consists of Sappho's effort to console her friend, as she had consoled Atthis (fragment 96), for the parting. The consolation takes the form of a list of pleasures formerly shared by the two lovers. And yet, as we see in the beginning line of the poem,

> . . . I wish in truth that I were dead,

Sappho is herself not consoled. As Denys Page says, about this line:

> . . . that was not said at the time of parting; it is what she says *now,* when she recalls the scene of parting and all that it means to her. At the time, she played the part of the stronger spirit, the comforter, in the presence of her distraught companion: today she avows a grief as great as her companion's, or greater.

It can be asked whether anything deeper is noticed here in Sappho than selected instants in her highly emotional existence. Isn't it simply that she, living in the sophisticated and relatively cosmopolitan society of sixth century Lesbos, was continually subject to comings and goings, and has recorded that experience in her poetry? Isn't Sappho spiritually cut off, say, from a poet like Archilochos? As Page writes:

> They (these girls) come from Miletus, from Phocaea, from Colophon, to live in Sappho's society; and one day they go away again.
>
> (*Sappho and Alcaeus,* p. 95)

As we know, however, poetry is always only a more or less indirect record of lived life. In the present case we could insist that Sappho's invocation-poems—those in which she invites the presence of Aphrodite or Hera—have no factual reality. Nor do they seem to be merely conventional. They are not simply Muse-inviting poems. Rather they correspond to some inner "intention" of the author. In the same way the dialectical treatment of pursuit and flight in fragment 1, discussed above, is clearly witty, is part more of a conceit than of a confession. Or the time-lag device of fragment 94, which contributed to the poignancy of that poem, was a transparently successful concession to artifice. In other words, it will do much less than complete justice to Sappho's poems to think of them as autobiographical records. The demand for attention to self, in the Greek lyric, does not express itself *that* directly.

I suggest that part of what we find in the pitifully small remainder of Sappho is the record of a strong, almost geometrical, inward "concern" with patterns of coming and going. It could not be said that the comings and goings in her verse are autobiographically explicable, though many of them probably are. Nor, at the opposite extreme, do those comings and goings express almost abstractly inward tensions, without much vital content. The truth lies between the poles. Sappho is inwardly disposed to experiences which fall into patterns of coming and departure. This inward disposition doubtless had roots in some ultimate erotic tendencies, such as those of inviting the world to her breast, and of dreading the trauma of losing the world. At the least Sappho's inward and deep disposition readied her to find suitable for her poetry such experiences, in all their vitality, as she has there embodied. In a sense she only experienced, and offered us, what she was. In that, she draws us back to the great empiricist of the poetry of her day; back to Archilochos.

Notes and References

Chapter One

1. The non-specialist feels increasingly shut out from the arcana of this new learning. Excavation reports in *The American Journal of Archaeology* or *Hesperia* are about as accessible, even to the classicist, as essays on astrophysics. We rely increasingly, for knowledge such as I summarize here, on books like those of A. R. Burn or Denys Page, which I have used heavily.

2. For more on this point, see the present author's "Objectivity in Homer." *Texas Studies in Literature and Language,* VII (1965).

3. M. I. Finley, in *The World of Odysseus* (New York, 1954), develops all these hints into a coherent, convincing whole.

4. For thorough commentary on this historical moment, cf. Burn, *The Lyric Age of Greece* (London, 1960).

5. This chapter in economic history needs to be rewritten. George Thomson's Marxist analysis, in *Aeschylus and Athens* (London, 1946) and the good book by P. N. Ure, *The Origin of Tyranny* (Cambridge, 1922) hold the field now. Both writers see deeply into the spiritual changes involved with the distribution of coinage. But many facts about Mediterranean culture have been learned since they wrote. And economic theory, Marxist included, has refined itself.

6. A good deal has been written on this harvest. On the blending of literature with speculative thought, at this time, there is special help in Cornford's *From Religion to Philosophy* (New York, 1912), in Hans Diller's article, "Hesiod und die Anfänge der griechischen Philosophie," *Antike und Abendland,* II (1949), and in metaphysical analyses like Stanley Rosen's in *Arion,* I (1962).

7. I have tried to discuss the meaningful complexity of Hesiod's position in "Observations on the Conflict of Art and Didacticism in Hesiod," *Symbolae Osloenses,* XXXVI (1961).

8. The standard and classical facts are best assembled, I think, in Hauvette's *Archiloque* (Paris, 1905). For the brand new inscriptional

material, not yet fully deciphered or interpreted, cf. the articles by Peek, *Philologus*, XCIX (1955) and Kontoleon, *Philologus*, C (1956).

Chapter Two

1. The kind of thought required to account for *this kind* of movement in history is rare. Karl Jaspers sets the model in his *Vom Ursprung und Ziel der Geschichte* (Hamburg, 1955), but restricts his best insights to the worldwide spiritual revolution of the fifth century B.C. The only candidate, for direct discussion of the metaphysics of the leap out of the epic world, is Eric Voegelin's *The World of the Polis* (Baton Rouge, 1957).

2. I only skirt the distinction between oral and written cultures. It is in fact of the vastest importance that Archilochos was living (as it seems) on the border between oral and written culture. The falling apart of the epic world, at his back, had more than incidentally been caused by papyrus paper and stylus pens. For a lyric disquisition on these implications, cf. Marshall McLuhan, *The Gutenberg Galaxy* (Toronto, 1962).

3. For more, cf. *The Decipherment of Linear B* (Cambridge, 1958) by John Chadwick.

4. Crusius, article on "Archilochos," *Realenzyklopädie der klassischen Altertumswissenschaft* (1895).

5. Fr. 23. References are to Bergk's text of Archilochos in his *Poetae lyrici Graeci* (Leipzig, 1915).

6. Homer, *Iliad*, I. 1–7.

7. For profitable use of the idea of "thingliness" as a critical concept, I am indebted to French critics like Bachelard, say, in his *La Psychanalyse du Feu* (Paris, 1949), to Ponge, or to Sartre, as in his studies of viscosity, in *L'Être et le Néant* (Paris, 1949).

8. There is a revealing comment on this by J. A. Symonds, in his *Studies of the Greek Poets* (New York, 1880), I, 280: "Greek sculpture is not more pure in outline than the following fragment, which sets before our eyes the figure of a girl embossed on marble or engraved in chalcedony . . ." I quote because of its period flavor. We might well wonder, today, whether the girl was an hetaira.

9. For more on these crucial, and little discussed, overtones of "sight" in Western culture, cf. Erwin Panofsky's *Meaning in the Visual Arts* (Garden City, 1955); De Bruyne's *L'Esthétique du Moyen Age* (Louvain, 1947); and my *Intelligible Beauty in Aesthetic Thought* (Tübingen, 1958). It is also worth considering a deflation of the pregnant notion of sight, during and after the Romantic movement, at which time, and until our day, the ear has taken over as the leading sense organ.

Chapter Three

1. Cf. various works by Bruno Snell and Max Treu for discussion of the simultaneous developments in *linguistic* and *cultural* history.

2. The issue touched here is far too ambitious for my present text, yet certainly one of the most important to arise directly and legitimately from it. Archilochos, I think, had a perfectly pre-Christian temper: of a natural goodness, capable of love, lacking the guidance of grace. For a phenomenology of that temper, in terms of cultural history, we still have nothing better than C. N. Cochrane's *From Christianity to Classical Culture* (Oxford, 1940).

3. Echoes, which even we can hear, abound in the lyric poets. Isn't it likely that a contemporary of Archilochos, hearing these lines, would have thought of Helen at the Skaian gates and her effect on the old men there? Thinking of what we do hear, like this, makes us doubly conscious of what we must miss.

4. I have tried, in "From Naming to Fiction-Making," *Giornale di Metafisica*, V (1958), 569–83, to develop this idea; that language inevitably moves away from what it names into the world of idea, or at least, a beginning of such "spiritualization" into that of syntax. Some attention should also be paid to the purely demonstrative function of language, even in its early stages of growth.

5. Max Treu's *Von Homer zur Lyrik* (Munich, 1955), makes a skillful assault on these problems in linguistic history. It is sometimes appalling to realize how little we know, not only about frequency of vocabulary in ancient Greek, but also about the ironies and levels of words, that is, in what kinds of mouth, and in what ways, they would have sounded appropriate.

6. I have steered away from the literary-historical meaning of this fragment, but there, obviously, its chief importance is lodged. Werner Jaeger, in *Paideia* (trans. Oxford, 1939–44), does fullest and most imaginative justice to the revolutionary implications.

7. A special advantage to the study of ancient literature is just this: that we are repeatedly forced to ignore chronology and to take a chance on essence. Obviously we lose something, a kind of intelligibility, in this way. But we gain immediacy and a new sense, which scholarship is forever trying to quell, of the pressure on us of the very existence of a literary work.

8. These erotic fragments are so wholehearted and clean. It is hard to decide when prurience got into Greek literature. We find virtually none in Homer or Hesiod and very little in the lyric poets. It is similarly lacking in archaic sculpture, of course. It makes perhaps its first literary appearance in Euripides: certainly in the *Bacchae* or *Hip-*

polytus it is obvious. But there is none in the remains (and copies) of fifth-century sculpture, in the Parthenon or Bassae figures, or in the finest Apolline statues. Archilochos seems far prior to whatever larger cultural neuroses expressed themselves in the fifth century.

Chapter Four

1. About as close as we can come to useful discussion of "literary ideas" is to be found in Yvor Winters' *In Defence of Reason* (Denver, 1947). Winters, I think, finds that literature "immoral" which does not develop at least some meaningfully isolatable ideas; and he would certainly be right to claim Plato as a partial ally. There is an excellent discussion of this point in Wellek and Warren, *The Theory of Literature* (New York, 1949), in the chapter on "Literature and Ideas."

2. Not always, fortunately; as there are fine studies like W. B. Stanford's *Ambiguity in Greek Literature* (Oxford, 1939) and *Greek Metaphor* (Oxford, 1936); or H. A. Musurillo's literary *Symbol and Myth in Ancient Poetry* (New York, 1961). Almost always, though, the critic must stop short of wit as it turns toward humor or play. That realm is always, it seems, the best-guarded sanctum of a language, though it is also, perhaps, the lair of a language's true genius.

3. It had best be reminded, here, that the Greeks of the time had no single word for "nature," in any of the senses we give it. We do translate their *physis* as "nature"; but its meaning was abstract, referring simply to "things which grow."

4. An equation reminding us of the very useful work which could be done on the idiom of metaphor in the Greek lyric poets; that is, a study of the physical symbols habitually chosen to bring out inner states.

5. Or as has been shown by R. Pfeiffer in an important article on divinity and the individual, *Philologus*, LXXXIV (1929).

Chapter Five

1. Dodds, on *The Greeks and the Irrational* (Berkeley, 1951), is vastly useful on the remnants of epic, face-saving ethic in the later world of Greek lyric.

Chapter Six

1. The topic of ancient literary influences, the influences of one ancient author on another, is extremely delicate, partly because so much has been lost, so that we must miss most of the resonances, but mainly because literary property in antiquity was much more public than it is today, indeed than it has been since the Renaissance, so that what might strike us as plagiarism is in fact, generally, the result of legiti-

mate emulation, what Milton called *aemulatio*. On this ancient perspective, cf. Fiske, *Lucilius and Horace* (Madison, 1920), and my "Publica Materies," *Arion*, II (1963).

2. Heraclitus, fr. 42 (I, 160, Diels-Kranz edition).

3. Treu prints, as the first of the "new discoveries" in his *Archilochos* (Munich, 1959), the text of a fictional debate between Homer and Archilochos, made up of quotations from the two authors, and taken from a third century B.C. papyrus. In his notes on the debate, pp. 174 ff., he assembles the other considerable evidence for pairing Homer with Archilochos.

4. Cf., for more analysis of the evidence, Philip Wheelwright, *Heraclitus* (Princeton, 1959).

5. *Pythian*. 2. 52 ff.

6. Critias, fr. 44, in Aelian, *Varia Historia*, X, 13.

7. This is one subject, for the classicist, which has been little touched, and should be further explored, for it goes to the heart of the way in which ancient Greece was an esthetic culture. On the definition of the *I*, in Greek culture, the best study is still J. Böhme, *Die Seele und das Ich bei Homer* (Göttingen, 1929); while my "The Concept of *Character* in Euripides," *Glotta*, XXIX (1960–61), looks at a particular, and important, feature of the question. The larger topic, of Greek literary self-awareness, comes up for occasional study in J. W. H. Atkins' *Literary Criticism in Antiquity* (Cambridge, 1934).

8. *Anthologia Palatina*, XI, 20.

9. *De Signis Temp*. 45.

10. Fr. 37 (Schneider's edition).

11. *Anthologia Palatina*, VII, 70.

12. *Anthologia Palatina*, VIII, 71.

13. First Tarsian speech: XXXIII, Vol. I, 330, 9 ff., ed. Arn.

14. *Imp. Misop.*, p. 433, ed. Hertlein.

15. Synesius, *De Insomnia* xx.

16. For more of the Greek evidence, see the careful résumé in Schmid-Stählin, *Geschichte der griechischen Literatur* (Munich, 1929), I, 1, 396.

17. *Epistula* i. 19. 22 ff. For more comments on Horace's indebtedness, see Fraenkel, *Horace* (Oxford, 1957).

18. Lasserre, *Les Épodes d'Archiloque* (Paris, 1950), makes an effort to show a detailed dependence of Horace on Archilochos.

19. *Ars Poetica* 79–82.

20. Epode V, 1–2.

21. Fr. 94 D (Treu).

Chapter Seven

1. This point is essentially confirmed in Brooks and Wimsatt, *Literary Criticism: A Short History* (New York, 1957).

2. Point powerfully elaborated by Marshall McLuhan in *The Gutenberg Galaxy*, cited above, Chapter 2, note 2.

3. *Vitae* ii. 27. 10.

4. Clement of Alexandria, *Stromata* i. 316.

5. Scholiast on Archilochos, fr. 275; cited in Lasserre, *Les Épodes d'Archiloque* (Paris, 1950), at relevant point in fragment list.

6. Lasserre, *Les Épodes*, lxxxvii.

7. *Ibid.*

8. This kind of linguistic-philosophic insight has been most satisfactorily developed for the English speaking and reading world by B. L. Whorff in his *Language, Thought and Reality* (Cambridge, 1956). His viewpoint has been elaborated into a major weapon both of literary criticism and of philosophical analysis.

9. For an exemplary study of such poetic nakedness, in modern verse specifically, but with wide extension, see Geoffrey Hartman, *The Unmediated Vision* (New Haven, 1954).

10. Jaeger, *Paideia* (Oxford, 1939), I, 114.

11. *Vita Nuova*, Canto XXXIX, translated by Mark Musa.

12. Fränkel, *Dichtung und Philosophie* (New York, 1951), p. 169. My translations.

13. *Ibid.*

14. *Ibid.*, note 240.

15. *Ibid.*, p. 156.

16. *Ibid.*, p. 191.

17. Cited by Staiger, *Grundbegriffe* (Zürich, 1946), p. 24.

18. *Ibid.*, p. 16.

Selected Bibliography

I include works which have been of particular use to me, and in most cases append a few descriptive or critical words. For a much more thorough bibliography, see Treu's *Archilochos*, which is listed below.

PRIMARY SOURCES

1. *Texts*

BERGK, THEODOR. *Poetae lyrici Graeci.* Leipzig: Teubner, 1915 (revised edition). The text I use for all fragments.

LASSERRE, F. and BONNARD, A. *Archiloque: Fragments.* Paris: Les Belles Lettres, 1958. Excellent literary critical introduction by Bonnard.

TREU, MAX. *Archilochos.* Munich: Heimeran Verlag, 1959. Good text; useful notes and essay on the poet.

2. *Translations*

DAVENPORT, GUY, with introduction by HUGH KENNER. *Carmina Archilochi; the Fragments of Archilochos.* Berkeley: University of California Press, 1964. Creative work. Contrives, by taking amazing risks, to establish an accurate sense of the quality of Archilochos' verse.

LATTIMORE, RICHMOND. *Greek Lyrics.* Chicago: University of Chicago Press, 1960. Contains a number of the best known poems.

SECONDARY SOURCES

1. *Books*

ADKINS, A. W. *Merit and Responsibility.* Oxford: Clarendon Press, 1960. On the central cultural change between Homer and fifth century; stressing, en route, the slow freeing of human values in the sixth century from the face-and-honor code of the epic world.

BEARE, J. *Greek Theories of Elementary Cognition from Alcmaeon to Aristotle.* Oxford: Clarendon Press, 1906. Timid and dated, but still proof (and about the only proof) of how much good work might be done in this direction, of analyzing fundamental "modes of awareness" among the Greeks.

BLUMENTHAL, A. VON. *Die Schaetzung des Archilochos im Altertume.* Stuttgart: Kohlhammer, 1922. A useful compilation of the matter, with analyses.

BÖHME, J. *Die Seele und das Ich bei Homer.* Unpublished Ph.D. dissertation, Göttingen University, 1929.

BOWRA, C. M. *Early Greek Elegists.* Cambridge, Mass.: Harvard University Press, 1938. Urbane, readable, guiding; but finally superficial.

BROWN, NORMAN O. *Hesiod: Theogony.* New York: Liberal Arts, 1953. Translation with introduction. Exemplary anthropological-theological analysis: full of hints for the classicist.

————. *Life against Death.* Middletown: Wesleyan University Press, 1959. An immense move out from the position of the classical scholar to commentary on human existence, while preserving insights won from experience of early Greek culture.

BURN, A. R. *The Lyric Age of Greece.* London: Edw. Arnold, 1960. Strongest effort made, so far, to integrate new archaeological-historical evidence about early Greece with literary criticism. Dense, crabbed reading.

————. *The World of Hesiod.* London: Kegan Paul, Trench, Trübner, 1936. Almost does for Hesiod what Finley (*q.v.*) did for Homer.

CORNFORD, F. M. *From Religion to Philosophy.* New York: Longmans, Green, 1912. Directly unconcerned with Greek poetry, but illuminating on the broad change of sensibility linking Homer to the Milesians, thus to the "new world" of lyric and philosophy.

DODDS, E. R. *The Greeks and the Irrational.* Berkeley: University of California Press, 1951. Not on the poems, but invaluable for a grasp of the thought world formed around them.

FINLEY, M. I. *The World of Odysseus.* New York: Viking Press, 1954. Deft and simple historical analysis, suggesting how well, in the right hands, something similar could be done about the world of Archilochos.

FISKE, G. C. *Lucilius and Horace.* Madison: University of Wisconsin, 1920. Classic study of the "classical theory of imitation."

FRAENKEL, EDUARD. *Horace.* Oxford: Clarendon Press, 1957. Discusses Horace's "debt" to Archilochos.

FRÄNKEL, HERMANN. *Dichtung und Philosophie des frühen Griechentums.* New York: American Philological Association, 1951. Touches all the early lyric poets, leaving no fragment undeepened.

FRYE, NORTHROP. *The Anatomy of Criticism.* Princeton: Princeton

University Press, 1957. Cannot now be sidestepped by anyone concerned with the nature of literary genres.

HARTMAN, GEOFFREY. *The Unmediated Vision*. New Haven: Yale University Press, 1954. Worthy of notice because of its epistemological method, which is carefully and deeply applied to some problems in modern poetry in a manner worth attention by critics of any poetry.

HAUVETTE, AMÉDÉE. *Archiloque, sa vie et ses Poésies*. Paris: Fontemoing, 1905. A comprehensive early study covering every aspect of the poet. Though now outdated, it is still readable, and essentially correct.

JAEGER, WERNER. *Paideia*. Translated by GILBERT HIGHET. 3 vols. Oxford: Blackwell, 1939. Much of value on Archilochos and on everything else in Greek culture.

LASSERRE, F. *Les Épodes d'Archiloque*. Paris: Les Belles Lettres, 1950. Ingenious (to me also bewildering and dubious) effort to reconstruct whole epodes of Archilochos on the basis of allusions and echoes of Archilochos in Horace.

LEO, F. *De Horatio et Archilocho*. Göttingen: Programm der Universität Göttingen, 1900. Pioneer study of this literary relationship.

LESKY, A. *Die Tragische Dichtung der Hellenen*. Göttingen: Vandenhoeck and Ruprecht, 1956. Helps indirectly toward understanding the lyric poets.

PAGE, DENYS. *History and the Homeric Iliad*. Berkeley: University of California Press, 1959. Especially useful for showing how new archaeological and linguistic studies can be applied to an understanding of the Near Eastern background of early Greek culture.

PAULY-WISSOWA. *Realenzyklopädie der klassischen Altertumswissenschaft* (RE), *Article:* "Archilochos" (by CRUSIUS), 1895. Long, dense article; still the best single scholarly guide to understanding the poet.

POHLENZ, M. *Die griechische Tragödie*. Berlin: Teubner, 1930.

POUILLOUX, J. *Archiloque: Sept Exposés et Discussions*. Geneva: Fondation Hardt, 1964.

ROHEIM, GEZA. *The Origin and Function of Culture*. New York: Nervous and Mental Disease Monographs, 1943. A post-Freudian analysis, with ample remarks on early Mediterranean cultures. Like N. O. Brown, listed above, and George Thomson, listed below, Roheim brings specifically and technically new understandings to old texts.

ROMILLY, JACQUELINE DE. *La Crainte et l'Angoisse dans le Théâtre d'Eschyle*. Paris: Presses Universitaires, 1958. A classic analysis, dwelling with great clarity on the Angst in Aeschylean drama. Could, I think, be usefully transferred to analysis of the lyric poets. (Perhaps first to the revealing question of "loneliness" in their work.)

SANDYS, J. *A History of Classical Scholarship.* 3 vols. Cambridge: Cambridge University Press, 1906–8. Standard survey. Dull, shallow, indispensable.

SCHMID, W. *Geschichte der griechischen Literatur.* Munich: Beck, 1929. Vol. I, part 1. Best single placing of Archilochos' poetry in its literary-historical context.

SNELL, BRUNO. *The Discovery of the Mind.* Translated by THOMAS ROSENMEYER. Oxford: Blackwell, 1953. The pioneering breakthrough, from viewpoints of linguistics and cultural history, into early Greek culture.

STAIGER, EMIL. *Grundbegriffe der Poetik.* Zürich: Atlantis Verlag, 1946. A classic of genre study. At its best on the lyric.

SYMONDS, JOHN ADDINGTON. *Studies of the Greek Poets.* New York: Harper & Bros., 1880. Lucid *fin-de-siècle* insights, sometimes particularly valuable, as in the study of Archilochos, when critical assumptions unlike our own are central.

THOMSON, GEORGE. *Aeschylus and Athens.* London: Lawrence and Wishart, 1946. The best Marxist analysis of early Greek civilization. Impossible to disregard his economic analysis of the "birth" of the post-epic world.

TREU, MAX. *Alkaios.* Munich: Heimeran, 1959. Translation and edition. Like Treu's *Archilochos* and the book listed immediately below: convenient, scholarly, literarily aware.

———. *Sappho.* Munich: Heimeran, 1958. Translation and edition.

———. *Von Homer zur Lyrik.* Munich: Beck, 1955. Linguistic-literary study of the development of early Greek poetry.

VOEGELIN, E. *The World of the Polis.* Vol. II of his *Order and History.* Baton Rouge: Louisiana State University Press, 1957. Mysterious, often too speculative, but persistently addressed to crucial questions, like why the polis emerged, which everyone must face in trying to analyze pre-fifth-century Greek culture. A courageous book.

WHEELWRIGHT, P. *Heraclitus.* Princeton: Princeton University Press, 1959.

2. *Articles*

(A brief sample of the rich material, much of which, collected around individual fragments, is too detailed to be appropriate here: for more, see bibliography in Treu's *Archilochos.*)

DILLER, HANS. "Hesiod und die Anfänge der griechischen Philosophie" ("Hesiod and the Beginnings of Greek Philosophy"), *Antike und Abendland*, II (1949), 140 ff. Pioneering study of interrelations between Greek myth and Greek philosophy.

KNOX, A. D. "The Early Iambos," *Philologus*, LXXXVII (1932), 18 ff. Examines the development of the iambic form.

KONTOLEON, N. M. "Zu den neuen Archilochosinschriften" ("On the New Archilochos Inscriptions"), *Philologus*, C (1956), 29 ff. Studies his own earlier newfound inscriptions concerning Archilochos and Paros.

PEEK, W. "Neues von Archilochos" ("New Material on Archilochos"), *Philologus*, XCIX (1955), 4 ff. Inscriptional material.

————. "Die Archilochos-Gedichte von Oxyrhynchos" ("The Archilochos Poems from Oxyrhynchos"), *Philologus*, XCIX (1955), 193 ff. Inscriptional material.

PFEIFFER, R. "Gottheit und Individuum in der frühgriechischen Lyrik" ("Divinity and the Individual in Early Greek Lyric"), *Philologus*, LXXXIV (1929), 137 ff. Good on the special nature of religious expression in Greek lyric. Sees more piety in Archilochos than is usually supposed.

ROSEN, STANLEY. "Thales," *Arion*, I (1962), 48–64. Included here as an example of a metaphysically coherent analysis of a fragmentary early Greek author.

SNELL, BRUNO. "Das Heitere im frühen Griechentum" ("Gaiety in early Hellenism"), *Antike und Abendland*, VI (1957), 149 ff. Studies early Hellenic "joyfulness."

————. "Zur Soziologie des archaischen Griechentums: Der Einzelne und die Gruppe" ("On the Sociology of Ancient Hellenism: The Individual and the Group"), 48 ff. Examines literary indications of relation between individual and society in early Hellenism.

WILL, FREDERIC. "Solon's Consciousness of Himself," *Transactions of the American Philological Association*, LXXIX (1958), 301–11. Analytical study of self-awareness in a Greek lyric poet.

————. "The Concept of *Character* in Euripides," *Glotta*, XXIX (1960–61), 233–38. Study of a word, and the presuppositions behind the use of it.

————. "Observations on the Conflict of Art and Didacticism in Hesiod," *Symbolae Osloenses*, XXXVI (1961), 5–14. Study of an intellectual conflict.

————. "Archilochos and his Senses," *Classical Journal*, LVII (1962), 289–96. Preparatory to the present book.

————. "Prometheus and the Question of Self-Awareness in Literature," *American Journal of Philology*, LXXXIII (1962), 72–85.

Studies projection of Aeschylus' self-awareness into one of his creations.

————. "Publica Materies," *Arion*, II (1963), 131–42. On the "hard" features of the classical tradition, as they appear in Milton.

————. "Objectivity in Homer," *Texas Studies in Literature and Language*, VII (1965), 5–15. On the depersonalizing effects of the early Greek epic tradition.

Index